BRIDGING THE GAP

Advance Praise

"*Bridging the Gap* is a fascinating read, part autobiographical, part self-help but all part of the personal journey of Author Glen Williams, who as a cop, rode the roller coaster of a life in Law Enforcement."

Randy Sutton, A nationally known expert and commentator on law enforcement issues, who has appeared on *FOX AND FRIENDS, THE ONE AMERICA NEWS NETWORK*, and is the Crime and Safety on air personality for *KTNV TV Las Vegas*. He is a retired police Lieutenant and is the founder of The Wounded Blue. He is a radio personality hosting *BLUE LIVES RADIO, THE VOICE OF AMERICAN LAW ENFORCEMENT* and has written three books, *THE POWER OF LEGACY, TRUE BLUE; TO PROTECT AND SERVE*, and *A COP'S LIFE, TRUE STORIES FROM BEHIND THE BADGE,*

"Glen Williams worked in law enforcement for over two decades and the job took a tremendous toll on him, both professionally and personally. He has compiled some of those experiences, along with the lessons learned, into this book so others may benefit from what he learned the hard way. Those in public service will relate to a lot of what he says. Those not in public service will gain valuable insight as to how to deal with challenges in their own lives. An easy read with a lot of helpful information."

Kevin Thacker, Sandy City Chief of Police (retired)

"In *Bridging the Gap* Glen Williams has provided both heart and soul into the struggles of today's law enforcement officer. Glens honest approach to the issues that officers face is both insightful and inspiring. As a 30-year law enforcement veteran I found this to be an excellent read for anyone who is currently serving or planning on becoming a police officer. I highly recommend *Bridging the Gap* and I want to commend Glen for opening up this important world for all to see."

Bobby Kipper, Executive Director, National Center for Prevention of Community Violence, 30 Year Law Enforcement Veteran

"Upon reviewing the written materials entitled, *Bridging the Gap; An Inside Look at Communication and Relationships in Law Enforcement*, written by Mr. Glen Williams, I found it well written, informative and feel it would be a benefit to those I've worked with over the past 30 years—those in law enforcement, security, and crisis intervention. I look forward to being able to share this material with many others in published form."

Kerry Gracey, (Shaolin Arts), Nationally known Martial Artist, business owner counselor, and trainer of law enforcement and security

BRIDGING
THE GAP
AN INSIDE LOOK AT COMMUNICATIONS
AND RELATIONSHIPS AFTER TRAUMATIC EVENTS

GLEN WILLIAMS

NEW YORK

LONDON • NASHVILLE • MELBOURNE • VANCOUVER

BRIDGING THE GAP
An Inside Look at Communications and Relationships After Traumatic Events

Published in New York, New York, by Morgan James Publishing. Morgan James is a trademark of Morgan James, LLC. www.MorganJamesPublishing.com

A **FREE** ebook edition is available for you
or a friend with the purchase of this print book.

CLEARLY SIGN YOUR NAME ABOVE

Instructions to claim your free ebook edition:
1. Visit MorganJamesBOGO.com
2. Sign your name CLEARLY in the space above
3. Complete the form and submit a photo
   of this entire page
4. You or your friend can download the ebook
   to your preferred device

ISBN 978-1-63195-568-6 paperback
ISBN 978-1-63195-569-3 ebook
Library of Congress Control Number:
2021904940

Cover Design by:
Rachel Lopez
www.r2cdesign.com

Morgan James is a proud partner of Habitat for Humanity Peninsula
and Greater Williamsburg. Partners in building since 2006.

Get involved today! Visit
MorganJamesPublishing.com/giving-back

To my Grandfather,

In remembrance of the many hours spent in your library watching you research and write. Watching you type with one finger on an old Underwood typewriter and mostly, of our conversations as I learned to read and love books.

TABLE OF CONTENTS

ACKNOWLEDGMENTS

I had no idea how much work goes into writing and publishing a book and would like to thank the following people who taught me, inspired me and put up with me, and made it possible. First to my grandfather, Robert McCaffree and my mother, Phyllis who encouraged a love of books as I spent hours in my grandfather's library starting as a young child and through adulthood. To my father, Al, who taught me English at the dinner table and reviewed my work. Thank you, Angie Fenimore and the fellow coaches of Calliope Writers who taught this rank novice how a book should be laid out. To those coaches who read through my work and offered suggestions for improvement. They taught me the process of writing, editing, creating, and assisted me in becoming an author. And yes, the magic does happen in the editing. Thanks also to Eschler Editing and especially to Heidi Brockbank, who saw the value, and offered incredible insights and turned the professional editing of this book into an educational, enjoyable experience that greatly improved my work. Thank you, Morgan James Publishing, for taking a chance on Bridging the Gap and for seeing my passion and societies need for this book. Most importantly, thank you to my wife, Deborah, who waited patiently as I worked in my office, for hours, often neglecting other responsibilities, who listened as I read through my work, and who encouraged, offered ideas, and supported me every step of the way as I excitedly told her where I was in the publishing process and where things were going. Love you, Babe.

CHAPTER 1

THE AWAKENING

I slowly began easing my way down the rugged, steep mountain, strewn haphazardly with a myriad of rocks, boulders, and trees. It was difficult to see on this cloudy, dark night as a misty specter filtered the light from the narrow sliver of moon. As I moved among the large pine trees, I labored and struggled under the heavy weight of the pack on my back, carefully placing one foot before the other to avoid slipping on the granite rocks coated with lichen and moisture from the dew. I breathed deeply and raggedly, trying to catch my breath as I neared the most difficult point of the long, arduous trek. The thin oxygen-starved air made it hard to breathe. A cloud of mist escaped my mouth as I exhaled in the chilly 9500' elevation. Suddenly, a shot rang out. Hearing the familiar reverberation of distant sound, I instinctively ducked. Something whizzed by, ricocheting off a nearby rock in a high-

1

pitched whine, thudding into the mountainside behind me. Suddenly, I heard the delayed, loud echoing boom of another long-distance rifle shot. I sensed it and instinctively threw myself to the ground, rolling away from danger. A bullet struck the ground where I had been. Where were the shots coming from? Why was someone shooting at me? I quickly scooted away in a near panic, slowed by the dead weight of my large pack. It shifted precariously with the sudden movement, pitching forward and taking me with it. I started to slide rapidly down the steep rock and pine-covered slope, into the dark, ominous void below.

What started as a mild slide soon turned into a violent, uncontrollable tumble. I stuck my foot out at a passing heap of boulders in a vain attempt to stop or slow my momentum. The tumble and roll only got worse as I jammed my heels into the mountainside. Nothing slowed me as the pitch got steeper, more rugged, and more jagged. I bounced from rock to tree and back again. I felt like I was in a washing machine stuck on spin cycle.

I couldn't see what was coming. My surroundings seemed to get darker, steeper, and my wild, crazy movement sped up. I had lost all control.

And then something changed. *Was it the noise?* Yes, the noise was gone, except for my ragged, gasping breath. *Was it the mountain and the rocks?* Yes, they were gone too. The uncontrolled tumble was gone, and everything felt smooth and even. *Was it the pain?* No, the pain was still there. *Was it the fear?* No, the fear was also there, intensified tenfold.

The realization hit me like a ton of bricks: I was in mid-air. I had tumbled off a steep cliff and was falling. Down, down, and further down. Toward what?

I struggled with my gear, my body, and my pain, attempting to get my feet below me as I continued falling headfirst. One principle I learned as a young man was to protect your head, land on your feet. As I struggled to get myself oriented through the pain and the fog in my head, I sensed something. It was so dark; I still couldn't see. What was I feeling? A coolness, almost a mist in the air. Mist. Water. Oh! With a last desperate movement, I violently wrenched my body around until it was straight. Straight, like an arrow. My feet hit the surface of a lake. In that nanosecond of awareness, I gasped deeply, taking in as much air as I could and plunged down, deeper, and deeper into the icy water. My brain started to scream at me. Who had shot at me? How far had I tumbled and crashed down the mountain through the rocks and trees? How far had I plunged off the edge of the cliff? How deep was I going down into the lake? Still, I continued down. My body started to ache as I held on to what little breath I had. *You are running out of air,* my mind screamed at me. How much longer could I survive?

I struggled to pull my arm out of the waterlogged strap of my pack and twisted to free myself of the extra weight, but it wouldn't budge. *You're drowning. You're about to pass out,* my mind whispered. My body ached, and I hurt so much. I just wanted it to stop. All of a sudden, my right foot hit something solid, and in an instinctive flash of survival and anger, my subconscious recalled some ancient survival training I had learned as a young teen: Push off, get to the surface, and breathe. Do it again. Extend your life, until you solve the problem. Get out of this jam. Live! Survive! Instinctively, I pushed as hard as I could.

After what seemed like an eternity, my head broke the surface of the water and I gulped deeply for the air I so desperately needed. I slowly, painfully, began sinking again. That stupid pack was so heavy. Why couldn't I get rid of it, and why was it so heavy? Why couldn't I open it? I don't even remember putting that much in there.

As I sank slowly in the frigid water of the mountain lake, a face floated by. A young boy that had drowned and didn't live even after I did CPR on him. Down, down, and down, and I pushed off again. Another deep, ragged breath and I slid down beneath the surface again. Another face drifted upward past me. A girl that had been shot and killed. Kick up, breathe, down again. Another face. A girl that had been hit by a train. Again, and again! Another and another. A multitude of faces. I was so tired. How many times could I push off? My foot touched bottom, and I automatically pushed again. This time my ascent seemed easier and lighter as I rose through the water. This time felt different.

I bolted upright in bed, every muscle like a knot, aching, drenched in sweat, and gasping for air. The pain, palpable in the dark. I sat rigid in my bed; the sheets soaked in a clammy pool of sweat. I had survived another night. That stinking backpack full of memories that haunted me. They were indelibly inked in my mind. The ghastly incidents I had seen and never shared. This job! It is time. Time to talk about these experiences and how they have affected me and my life. Time to tell my wife.

Except I had built a wall of silence, one brick at a time. I was divorced. I was alone. What could I do?

CHAPTER 2

I WISH I HAD LISTENED

In the mid 1990s, Dr. Kevin M. Gilmartin, PhD, a retired deputy sheriff and experienced law enforcement clinician, presented an Emotional Survival for Law Enforcement workshop to Sandy City Police, where I worked at the time.

This was mandatory training. Through the efforts of people like Dr. Gilmartin, law enforcement was beginning to take a look at how to address the emotional baggage created by "the job." At the time, this emotional damage to officers was taken for granted, and little concern was shown for the high rates of divorce and the high suicide rates, which were very much under-reported and still seen in today's law enforcement world. I personally contributed to the divorce rate—even after hearing Dr. Gilmartin. I get to take personal accountability for that. At the time, I did not see how what he taught applied to me. This book is my personal journey, down the rabbit hole and through the steps that Dr. Gilmartin describes in his book. I could have been the model for his script. I also share some of the steps I discovered to find balance in my life. I share this information in the hopes that some other officer, whether young and idealistic or old and jaded, can learn from my experience.

I hope I can help you save a marriage or preserve a life. Maybe I can help you discover a way to balance your life and have good, strong relationships with family and friends. After all, even though law enforcement is critical and very important, it's just a job. It is not your life.

For most law enforcement professionals, the start of their journey is a time of positivity and excitement. The job application usually consists of a series of written and physical tests, as well as oral board interviews. This testing can vary, depending on the agency, but I have found it is fairly consistent throughout the country. While testing can be highly stressful, for most applicants, it's a positive experience with a new world to look forward to and new goals to reach. It is a moment to be proud of, when one is selected from, as in my case, several hundred applicants. After the hiring process comes the academy. Once again, the cadet faces a series of daily written, physical, and cognitive tests that last for several months. The training is rigorous, but the excitement of a new career helps the cadets through the endless hours of lectures, physical fitness preparation, testing, emergency vehicle response training, firearms training, and patrol technique training. The four to six months in the academy seem to pass in just a few days. Even though cadets may be exhausted, they are eager to face this new world.

These early experiences in the academy begin to shape the cadets' view of the law enforcement world. The experiences that come up in field training reshape their view of the world, their view of their role in law enforcement in that world, their view of the department, other cops, and most importantly, of themselves. However, as one of my original field training officers said, "Forget all the junk you learned in the academy—now it's time to learn the real world."

I soon figured out that the things taught in the academy were very idealistic. Now I looked to the older officers to teach me the ropes. I came to rely on them, and they pushed me to make sure they could rely on me. I soon found that I focused so much on surviving at work, I didn't keep up with old friends. I still participated in cherished activities like scuba diving and teaching, but on many occasions even those activities were pushed to the back burner. Over the first two years of my career everything was pushed aside as I pursued the goal to become a solo patrol officer.

I went from being very confident and idealistic, to being torn down and stressed-out during field training. I loved the job. The job didn't tear me down. Instead, the negative relationship with my training officers and the way some of them put me in lose/lose situations created undue stress. I recognized this because I was a thirty-two-year-old recruit with some life experience, not a wet-behind-the-ears twenty-one-year-old recruit. Knowing this didn't make it any easier. I originally figured I could survive field training, but soon I was hanging on by the tips of my fingers, just hoping for something good to happen. This was the start of my descent from motivated, idealistic rookie to jaded officer. Too often, becoming an experienced officer means becoming cynical, negative, and even angry. Becoming isolated and distant. I was fortunate not to have journeyed to the extreme end of the spectrum, but I came close on more than one occasion. I learned not to trust certain groups of officers, and there were times I was bitter as I witnessed the way other recruits were treated and saw it was not the same way I was being treated. It appeared to me that they were instantly accepted by their training officers. This made me work harder to be accepted, but I failed even more. In response, I distanced myself from my training officers, thinking the less I said the better. I stepped away from other officers as I was unsure who to trust. I also distanced myself from my wife, as I didn't want to burden her with my problems. I had been taught as a young man that I handle problems on my own. I went through the journey of idealism to distrust very quickly.

Once on my own as a solo officer, I was able to rebuild myself and regain the confidence I had lost. I was also able to rebuild my relationship with my wife. Then my real law enforcement journey began. This book is about my journey from idealistic, happily married recruit, living through the ups and downs of the job, and how I let the job take over my life. I'll share how I went from building the walls that led to two divorces, to eventually finding out how to remove the bricks in those walls. My life is now about learning to open up and be an idealistic, experienced officer. To be the best officer I can be, serving my community the way it deserves, and maintaining a good relationship with my wife and family.

This book was originally written for law enforcement professionals, but I have learned there are similar experiences in many other professions in our world. This book is for all public safety personnel, whether you are in patrol, detectives, records division, dispatch center, fighting fires or serving in an ambulance. It is for the medical professionals, especially those in the ER; for social workers, teachers, and those in our military; and for anyone experiencing trauma and possibly struggling with communication or relationships in their life. I want to share these experiences with you, in the hopes that you may learn from my mistakes and not make the same ones. The communication techniques I will present in this book can help reduce the onset of PTSD that many officers accumulate through the years. This will assist in reducing the divorce rate and suicide rate that is so high in these professions.

Please learn from the experiences I have had. Learn to communicate and to speak up for yourself and your relationships with your families and friends.

CHAPTER 3

IN THE BEGINNING

Many issues we face in life and in our career are based on experiences, preconceptions, judgments, and beliefs that are fostered early in life. These things come back later in life to affect many decisions we make. The following experiences in my early life formed some of the beliefs and preconceptions that I learned. My early experiences affected some of the choices I made in situations and relationships later in life.

I worked for the U.S. Postal Service from 1985 to 1991 as a letter carrier. During that time, I applied for the U.S. Postal Inspection Service, a Federal Law Enforcement Agency that investigates mail fraud and other crimes that use the U.S. Postal Service for illegal means. When I was ready to apply, I asked the recruiter if having diabetes was a problem. I was told it was not but was informed that a college degree was required. I went back to school for two years, working full time during the day and going to the university full time at night. I finished my college degree to qualify and passed all of the required application tests for the Postal Inspection Service. The last step before being hired was filling out the medical review. I checked yes on the box indicating diabetes.

You can imagine my dismay when I received a declination letter a few weeks later which stated:

1. Because of your diabetes we do not feel you can manage the strenuous physical activity required for this job.
2. Because of your diabetes we do not feel you can manage the arduous hours required in this job.

I met with the new recruiter for the Postal Inspection Service to ask about this decision, because it was opposite of what I had been originally told. During our discussion, she asked me a couple of questions.

"What would you do if you were on an all-night surveillance?

I answered, "I would keep a cooler of food in my car along with my insulin."

Her follow-up question was, "What if you were outside, by a light post, and not in a car?

"I would throw a candy bar and my insulin in a pocket and have enough sugar on me to get through."

"What if you were by that light post and couldn't leave for 48 hours?"

The unrealistic scenarios presented in her questions and her demeanor told me it didn't matter what I said. She was not going to consider changing the decision. Since it didn't matter, I brutally and honestly responded, "You don't plan your surveillance very well, do you?"

I talked to three attorneys about discrimination, because I was confident of support from the Americans with Disabilities Act, only be told, that at that time, the Federal Government was exempt from its own law. I later learned that the law was so new, no one wanted to challenge it yet. Either way, I would not be hired and couldn't fight it.

My diabetes had never been a problem in the past. It had never hindered or prevented me from doing any job or activity, although I once had to lie about it so I could learn to scuba dive. Being pigeonholed caused me to think back over my life and the experiences I had with diabetes.

I developed type 1 (juvenile diabetes) when I was fifteen years old. This challenge was a life changer for me. Even though I didn't really understand it, I decided to move forward and beat it down. At that time, there wasn't as much information about diabetes. Being young and not really understanding the disease, I resisted all of the eating restrictions my mother and doctors put on me. I simply ignored my problem. Later in life, as medical technology improved, I learned to manage things better. I found there were a lot of barriers for diabetics. While in college I wanted to take a course in scuba diving. I already had a heavy academic load with chemistry, physics, and English and needed an easy two-credit course to keep my student loans. Scuba diving was it. I lied about having diabetes because in 1981, diabetes was an automatic disqualifier from any scuba diving course. After completing the course, I was certified as a scuba diver. I loved diving so much that I quickly moved up the certification ladder, eventually becoming a scuba diving instructor in 1982. Once again, in order to participate in an activity, I loved and was fully capable of doing, I had to hide the fact that I had diabetes. I finally found a doctor in 1986 who encouraged all of her patients to live the life they wanted. She supported me and other people with diabetes participating in activities like scuba diving. This doctor supported my training to complete a 560-mile bicycle ride in three days. My objective was to raise money for diabetes research and to show that people with diabetes can do anything a "normal" person can. That ride was completed in 1989. Unfortunately, a couple of years later, this doctor was forced to retire for health reasons and later succumbed to cancer.

———————

Once again, despite the twist in my life of diabetes, I learned that hard work could overcome the judgment of others. By 1996 diabetes was no longer a disqualifying factor for scuba diving but did require a doctor's release to participate. I applied to become an instructor trainer in scuba diving. I met all of the requirements but needed the required medical release to be accepted into the course. I went to the partner of my former doctor, which turned out to be a mistake: He informed me he would not sign the release. This doctor did not feel diabetics should do things like scuba diving. I immediately told him that this patient did not feel he should be my doctor and replaced him with a new doctor who was not afraid to sign the medical release. Once I received that release, I was allowed to take the course. After completion, I was in the top 1 percent of scuba diving instructors in the nation and one of the top three ranked instructors in the state of Utah.

In the application process for the Postal Inspection Service, diabetes had reared its ugly head again, and this time I could not ignore it or lie about it. This time the rules beat me and completely shifted the direction of my life. I had finally figured out what I wanted to do with my life, but diabetes was an automatic disqualifier for admission into Federal Law Enforcement.

WHAT DO I DO NOW?

One night as I was teaching scuba diving, I expressed my frustration to a fellow instructor, who happened to be the supervisor over the district attorney's investigative team. He said, "Hey, Sandy City Police Department is hiring, why don't you apply there?"

I talked to my wife about it, and she agreed with him and said I should apply. I wanted to be in law enforcement, there was no chance to move up where I was at in the post office and being a letter carrier was not fulfilling to me. This began my journey toward being a "local cop." I applied to the Sandy City Police Department. The testing process was pretty standard for the time: a written test, a physical test, an interview, a pre-hire polygraph, and a psych test.

Once again, diabetes threatened to be a possible deterrent when I checked in for the 1.5-mile run portion of the physical test. I gave my name to the sergeant at the track and his response was, "Oh, you're the one with diabetes; they might not hire you." That was the wrong thing to say to a highly competitive, motivated person. The mile and a half took 6 laps at the local high school track, and we had to complete in a time under 15 minutes. As I crossed the finish line around the eleven-minute mark, almost a lap ahead of my nearest competitor, I looked at the sergeant and simply said, "Now try not to hire me!"

I was hired by Sandy City in May of 1991, but there was not an opening at the Peace Officer Standards and Training Academy until August, so I was allowed to work as a desk officer until I went to the academy.

The Academy was an interesting experience. Thirty competitive, mostly type-A personalities were working through the process. There were awards for outstanding officer, fitness, firearms, and academics. They were all based on our daily performances. I was competent enough, but I didn't realize back then that I hid my insecurities by overachieving. The result was that I appeared arrogant. I answered questions and spoke up, sometimes out of turn. My answers were correct, but my methods and mannerisms irritated some people. I was very goal oriented and was among the top five candidates academically. We had access to everyone's scores since they were posted daily. I was number one with a 97.5 percent average, and the next four students were all above 96 percent. I figured out that if I got a 97 percent on the final exam, I would be the top student. I got a 98 percent and earned the academic achievement award for maintaining the highest test scores throughout.

As part of our training, we ran several miles every day, along with other physical activities. On one run, a few days before our final qualifying tests, I stepped off a curb and severely sprained my ankle. Needless to say, my times were slower than normal, and I missed getting a fitness award by two percentage points. The last run was the "pride" run. This was a five-mile run that was not required but was intended to build teamwork and celebrate the end of the academy. I hobbled my way to the finish line. Again, I worked hard and pushed myself, just as I had learned when I was younger.

We had one two-hour training block in the police academy on family relations. Our spouses were invited to attend this section. We were told that 30 percent of us would get divorced. As I later learned, that was a low estimate. We were told that to avoid divorce, we should foster interests and hobbies outside of and not similar to law enforcement. We were also encouraged to invest financially so we could survive when we retired. One of the topics that was covered was communication with our spouses. Basically, we were told that as officers we should not talk much, since there were things that could not be shared or that we would not want to share. We were then told to make sure to keep communication open with our spouse, but no one told us how. We were just told that we couldn't or shouldn't share some things. Talk about unhelpful.

Law enforcement still maintains that closed-off frame of mind. Different movements in society today (including Black Lives Matter and anti-police politics) unfortunately strengthen the belief that opening up and allowing ourselves to be vulnerable is weak. That transparency is bad. The interesting thing is that transparency works, as long as what we are doing works for society.

The same is true in a family community. When I was a new officer, I shared everything with my wife. As I gained experience, moved to detectives, and dealt with negative politics at work, I shared less and less. Finally, all I did was work at the police department, along with two or three part time jobs, in the guise of taking care of my family. Our communication disappeared and my wife became depressed. Work became my escape.

CHAPTER 4

A ROCKY START

After the Academy came field training. Stress and more stress. My field training experience was not pleasant. In fact, it was downright brutal and something I have never forgotten. My first night on the job, I met my primary field training officer. For the next several months, he would hold absolute power and would rule my life, my feelings, and my future. The first thing he did was to put me in a small, dark room and order me to sit. The only seat available was a hard plastic chair. I later learned it was the suspect chair in the interview/interrogation room. He started yelling at me. One statement he made stuck with me: "You have the reputation around here as a cocky, arrogant know-it-all, and I'm going to change that." Unfortunately, it was downhill from there. I had been in the academy for months and was racking my brain to figure out what I had done or said and to whom, to have earned that reputation. Twenty years later, when I retired, I was given a copy of my academy paperwork, my rook book, and other paperwork from my personnel file. I discovered that the comment came from one of my fellow academy recruits who had said those things about me in the post-Academy comments. It was simply one person's impression, but I learned a brutal lesson in how one comment can almost destroy a career, and a life, as my entire field-training experience was based on that one comment. No matter what I did during field training, I was criticized. I was given barely passing scores or failed. One night, I was working a graveyard shift. It was cloudy, dark, and several degrees below freezing. It had started snowing heavily, making it impossible to see more than a few yards in front of me. There was already six to eight inches of snow on the ground, and it was icy and slick. We were dispatched to a burglary in a subdivision in one of the East Bench neighborhoods. The area known as the East Bench follows along the mountains on the east side of the Salt Lake valley. Most of the neighborhoods are upper middle class and overlook the cities located at elevations below. I approached the area, driving carefully. The car struggled to gain traction on the icy roads. I weaved my way up the hill to the subdivision, sliding side to side like a sewing machine in zig-zag mode. We stopped a few houses away from the victim's home, in case the suspects were still nearby. We approached on foot, making a pathway through the deep snow as we neared the home. Arriving at the front door, we saw three fresh sets of footprints leaving the front porch, going into the yard, and disappearing down the street in the opposite direction we had come from. The snow was coming down so fast and heavy, I was worried it would cover the footprints, so I immediately followed them, with my training officer trailing along, watching me. I remembered my training from the academy and made sure I stayed to the side of the prints, so I didn't obliterate them. The tracks continued on for about a block and a half before they angled into a yard and disappeared into the window well of a basement window located on the front of the home toward the right side. We approached and knocked on the front door of a nice upper-middle class, two-story home. A middle-aged woman answered the door. I asked her if there was anyone in the basement, and she told me her son and a couple of his friends were there. I asked her if they had been out that night, and she replied that they had been home all-night playing games in the basement. I asked her if she was sure of that, and pointed at the footprints in the snow, disappearing into the window well of her basement. The smile on her face disappeared and she naturally became worried, with two uniformed police officers on her front porch, braving the frigid elements and asking questions. She called the boys upstairs, and they slowly came up and froze in shock when they saw police officers. They had removed their shoes, but their stocking feet were still wet from the snow and their faces still flushed red from the cold. With that evidence, and mom's insistence, they confessed, and we recovered the property stolen from the neighbor's house up the street. I was grateful for a parent who taught her son and his friends to take accountability for their actions.

My field training officer gave me a failing score for that call. He explained that I followed the tracks on foot when I could have followed them in the car, and I didn't cover or protect the footprints at the scene to preserve them as evidence. Unfortunately, this was a repeating theme for the remainder of my field training. It felt to me that no matter what I did, I was going to receive a failing score, and that proved to be the case. I loved the job, but nothing I did satisfied my training officer.

Another incident really scared me. My field training officer was concerned that he had never seen me in a physically confrontational situation and wasn't sure I could handle one. On this spring night, my training officer and I were dispatched to a fight in progress at one of the local parks. It was another graveyard shift, dark but fairly warm. We arrived at the park and saw three guys milling around under the trees in the middle of the park. They were twenty or thirty yards from the parking area, away from the lights of the parking lot and in the shadows of the overhanging trees. We approached on foot, and I saw they looked like bodybuilders. All three were over six feet tall, very defined and muscular, and weighed between 220 and 250 pounds each. They were wearing tight Levi's and workout shirts that appeared to be stretched to the breaking point at the seams. The men seemed to be in a disagreement and arguing, jostling, and yelling at each other. These behemoths matched the suspect description given by dispatch. As I approached on foot, I gave verbal orders for them to separate and stop what they were doing. All three turned at the same time and moved toward us aggressively, as if ready to attack. I stepped back and again ordered them to stop. They continued to ignore the orders with sneers on their faces. I realized they were not going to stop and were getting closer than I felt was safe. I knew there was no way I could handle three large, muscular, athletic guys in a physical altercation so I drew my weapon, pointed it at them, and ordered them to get on the ground. They still did not stop and kept advancing forward together. All of a sudden, behind me, I heard my training officer's voice loudly yell, "Out of role, out of role," and the three males stopped. These were friends of my training officer from the gym, and he had staged this incident without telling me. I was furious at my trainer's deception and sick inside, because I could have shot or hurt someone. Again, I had been set up. and he gave me a failing score.

This was an ongoing pattern and really was stressful at the time. My training officer presented himself as in charge of the field training program, as if he ran everything. This took away any hope of reprieve for me. He was part of a group of officers who hung out together and were very close. Some of them had other recruits, and I watched as those recruits were accepted and how they passed, even while doing the same things I was failed for. This caused me to doubt myself, but my response was to try harder to be accepted. It only resulted in me failing harder.

I quickly became a little cynical. On my way to work each night, I wondered what booby trap my FTO would come up with, and what he would say to justify failing me again. I felt like I did not belong, and it was painfully obvious that I was not accepted.

I was deeply stressed. I only wanted to do a good job, to please and pass. Yet deep down, I knew there was nothing I could do that would be acceptable. Now I went into survival mode, because my field training officer was in a position to determine my future and career. It was a game, trying to figure out what he wanted me to do, and shift my methods to fit what he wanted. He wanted me to be more forceful and harder, so I was, only to get marked down in my scores for being too hard. Next, I was told I needed to be more empathetic. I willingly complied and was marked down for being too soft. Once I was marked down and failed because when I changed lanes in my patrol car, I clicked the turn signal up instead of just holding it so it would release when my lane change was complete. I was miserable, especially about not being accepted. I no longer had a solid base of who I was, since I was trying to change daily to be what my FTO wanted me to be—which kept changing. The very fabric of who I was, was being shredded, and not for any valid or beneficial reason. I had no confidence and no base left to return myself to. I was like a ship adrift, blowing back and forth, whichever way the winds were blowing. I didn't trust myself or anyone else as I got negative treatment, no matter what I did.

After several months of this "training", my training officer failed me from the field training program. I was distraught. Now what? I had already quit my other job. I was called into the chief's office. As I walked into his office he asked, "How are you?"

I responded in almost a whisper, "I don't know. I guess I'm out of a job."

The chief looked at me and simply said, "Let's talk about that."

We talked for a while and he then said, "Tell me about a good experience you had in your field training.

I hesitantly responded, "There really weren't any."

"There were no good experiences?" he asked.

"No, sir."

"Tell me about your best experience then."

I don't remember what I said, but after several seconds of thought that felt like an eternity, I related some minor experience.

His jaw dropped, and he asked incredulously, "That was your best experience?"

"Yes, sir"

He told me, "It sounds like you got into a negative spiral, and it just kept getting worse and worse, and there was no way for you to get out of it."

The chief thought for a few minutes, then came up with a plan he felt would work. The first part of the plan was removing my training officer from the field training officer program for a year. Then he had me transferred from patrol to a desk officer position. He let me go on the street with other patrol officers whenever I wanted and let me know that when I felt ready, I could go through field training again with different training officers. I worked at the front desk for about six months and went out on the street two or three times a week with different officers. I learned a lot and slowly regained my confidence.

Life continued on as normal for my wife and me, but there was a lot more stress in law enforcement than in the post office. Graveyard shifts present their own type of stress, both physical and mental. (Our bodies are designed to function better in the daylight hours, and working a graveyard shift also isolates us from family and community.) My stress was compounded by the negative situation with my field training officer and his associates. There was never any good news. I knew I could do this job, and I enjoyed the work, but no matter what I did, I was always told I had done it wrong and given poor scores.

Not again, I thought, *I got that right. How do I tell my wife how badly everything is going? How do I tell her I might not have a job? How do I pay the bills if I don't have a job? How do I tell her I am really worried? Don't stress her! She's had one miscarriage, and now she has the baby. Just try to get some sleep.* These were the thoughts I had as I struggled through field training. Not honestly sharing my fears and concerns were the first bricks I put in the wall. I stopped sharing, and looking back, I realize this was the beginning of the end of my marriage. My lack of communication was an additional stress on my wife and added to her postpartum depression. Her depression deepened, which only magnified the problem. I started showing signs of stress with sleep deprivation, and we started to argue a lot more. As I look back now, the negative spiral at work had invaded my family. We didn't know much about depression back then, or how to deal with it, but I know now how my wife's depression and my stressful situation at work was affecting my family life. I also know now that not talking about it didn't solve anything but actually made things worse. Unfortunately, that was the road I chose. I quit talking and followed the steps in Dr. Gilmartin's course and his book, *Emotional Survival for Law Enforcement.* These steps as explained by Dr. Gilmartin start with the positive, enthusiastic rookie who throws himself into the job, giving up other aspects of his life. He then begins building police relationships with other cops, forgoing the friendships of his previous life. This leads to emotional changes, which lead to physical changes including anger and emotional isolation, which lead to cynicism. In my case, I put so much energy into saving my job that I gave up all of my friends. At the same time, I had no one I trusted in the police department.

At work, my perspective had changed. Not about the local citizens but about the officers I worked with. I didn't trust them, and now

I didn't trust myself. Because I didn't trust myself, I shut down and became afraid to make decisions, even normal everyday ones at home. I distrusted myself so much that I couldn't even talk about it, thinking inside, "What if I say the wrong thing?" I didn't want to argue, I didn't want to discuss, and I didn't trust myself to speak. This was a pattern that would continue to create problems in my life.

CHAPTER 5

DESK OFFICER

While working at the desk one day, I struck up a conversation with an officer and decided to take advantage of the chief's offer to go out and ride with this officer. We were dispatched to a location where a man in his twenties had threatened to hurt his neighbors and had even threatened to shoot them. This man supposedly had a bunch of firearms in his house.

We approached and were about two houses away from the home when we could see the suspect in his front yard, yelling and screaming at no one in particular. He seemed very amped up and was provoked by anything he saw. He saw and recognized our marked patrol car, and that really set him off. At that point, we realized it wouldn't do any good to walk up, so we drove up to the corner of the property at the curb near his mailbox with the passenger side (my side of the car) closest to the yard.

He turned and started to run for the house. I immediately thought, *there is no way I am letting you get to the house with weapons,* and I jumped out of the car and ran after him. My partner was a big guy and had to negotiate from behind the steering wheel and around the car, so he was a little behind me. As the suspect neared the front porch of his home, I tackled him. Down on the ground, he twisted and squirmed to get away. I had my body on his back and shoulders and wrapped my arms around him in an old wrestling hold so he couldn't grab any weapons, if he had any. While he struggled, I attempted to force his arms behind his back to put handcuffs on him. Suddenly I felt a thud, and the suspect huffed and went limp. My oversized partner had caught up and jumped on the struggling suspect, landing on his waist, stomach, and legs, driving the air from his lungs. After that, it was easy to get the cuffs on the suspect, who no longer had any air or fight in him. As he sat there on the steps of the front porch, hands cuffed behind his back, recovering his breath, he asked, "Who tackled me first?" I answered, "I did." He sneered in an attempt to be tough and said, "I was running to get my rifle from my house. It's a good thing I didn't want to hurt you because I'm a black belt in karate and could have kicked you and broke your leg." I just looked at him, thinking to myself, *Dude, you are so full of it, but I'll let you have your ego and tell yourself you were nice and that is the only reason you got caught.* Outwardly, I simply responded, "I'm glad no one got hurt", and let it go. I had already learned that it does no good to get into a discussion on another person's ideas versus the reality of the situation.

I had several similar experiences during this time where I ended up in a physical confrontation with a suspect. This was the very thing my original field training officer wanted but didn't witness. A lot of the officers liked going out with me and trusted me. They knew that if they got in a physical altercation, they could count on me to back them up all the way. Some would even come in off the road during the day and ask me if I wanted to get away from the desk, so I could go out on patrol with them. I appreciated them as my confidence returned, and I grew as an officer. I was still nervous about work and having a job but was beginning to feel better about it.

CHAPTER 6

THE CLOWN

When I started field training again, my original training officer demanded that he be allowed to have input, but thankfully that demand was turned down by the chief. My original FTO and a couple of his friends still tried to have input by complaining to my new training officer about the way I handled several calls. They seemed determined to have me washed out. Other people (like the chief of police) were watching, but at this point I felt I only had one option: Don't make any mistakes. Be honest and stand up for myself.

One example was a civil custody dispute we were called on. A couple was separated and getting divorced. The father and his daughter were at his parent's house. The wife showed up at 2300 hours (11 p.m.), demanding to take her daughter. She had no paperwork, nothing from the court about custody, so I refused to remove the daughter from that home. My backup officer, one of my original training officers, demanded that I go in and forcibly remove the daughter, but I refused. My new training officer pulled me aside and asked why I was making that decision. I explained my reasoning to him, pointing out that without legal paperwork, I did not have the authority to remove the daughter. If I did so without the proper paperwork, I would be violating the law myself. The backup officer kept arguing about it, but my training officer stood up for me, told him I was correct, and told him to back off. My new field training officer was a good example of honesty and integrity.

This time, I did so well that the chief and my training officer felt I should be accelerated through the training program. But because of being failed on my first field training experience, there were potential liability issues. I had to go through the entire process again. I understood the reason why, but it felt like being in the 8th grade again, when my father was coaching me in football. I had played center on offense and linebacker on defense, even though I was not very big. My father talked to me after practice one day saying, "You are the best center on the team and the best linebacker, but because you are my son, I can only let you play one position." Of course, I chose linebacker. And in this training case, I chose to be loyal to the chief who had gone out on a limb for me, and I completed the entire field training process again. The department was just like the small town I grew up in, where accusations of favoritism were often heard. I learned early to work harder and give more than others to validate my position on the team, and in this case, I worked hard to validate my position in the department.

———————

Another experience stood out during this time. As we patrolled the city, my training officer would hear a call on the radio and volunteer us to take it if he thought it might turn into either something educational for me or a stressful situation to see how I handled it. One night a call was broadcast of a dead body. A few minutes later my training officer's phone rang, and he said we should go to that call. We arrived at the scene and saw several police and fire vehicles. Officers were outside a basement entry door at the front of the house. My training officer told me to hurry and took me to the entry doorway. As we walked up, he told me I was taking this call. As I approached the door, I saw that it was open a few inches. I asked if anyone had been inside yet and the officer at the door told me, "No, the door is blocked." As I got closer, I could see a red puddle covering the floor, through the narrow opening. It was blood, a lot of blood. As we eased the door open with slight pressure, I could see the victim lying on his back on the floor in a narrow hallway, his head and shoulders slumped against the wall opposite the door. One of his feet was against the door. There was a shotgun lying on the victim's chest with the barrel just under his chin. The wall behind the victim was red, as was the hallway and portions of the room behind him. The victim's head was missing from the ears up, and was a bloody, gory mess. The smell of blood was intense, overpowering the senses. The visual scene was even worse with blood and brain tissue covering everything. It appeared obvious and was later proven that he had placed the shotgun in his mouth before pulling the trigger. As we conducted our investigation, we found blood and brain tissue on the ceiling, floor, chairs, books, bookshelves and even the walls behind the books on the shelves. After finishing at the scene, the other officers took me to a local Italian restaurant and ordered lasagna for dinner. It looked similar to the mess we had just seen. I knew I was being tested and just commented on how good the lasagna was and added I would like more, even though I did not feel like eating at all.

───────────

These two field training experiences taught me a lot about precon-ceptions, judgment, and leadership. Many people in the department at that time were similar to my first training officer. It was their way or the highway. If someone did not fit into their mold, they were ostracized. For a long time after this, I had a real problem with trusting certain members of the cliques in the department. I knew they would do their job and do it well. I just didn't know if they would try to get me in a jam because they didn't like me. It made me very apprehensive and nervous to be around the guys that had tried to get me fired, and there was more than one attempt by them to have me removed from the department. I was constantly looking over my shoulder. Because of that, I was always on edge when they were around. Regardless, I made it through field training and was finally a solo officer. I hated politics, and even though I was a solo officer, there were other attempts by this particular group of officers to have me fired or disciplined. It really became nerve-racking when they and their friends moved up the chain of command, making sergeant and lieutenant. I originally wanted to go into certain specialized groups, like SWAT or K9, but never applied because I was not going to put myself into a position where any of them had any power over me. I didn't trust them, because I already knew what they would do. That distrust negatively influenced my career and marriage for a long time. I didn't realize it at the time, but it takes a lot of strength to work in a toxic or hostile work environment. There are no easy solutions. At this point in my life, I didn't have the emotional or communication skills to do anything about it. What I continued to do was work as hard as I could. I was determined to do the best job that I could and be as positive as I could.

At the time I took this behavior personally, but I have since learned it was not personal and that there are more productive ways to deal with malicious people at work. It doesn't matter if they are coworkers, bosses, or colleagues. This kind of situation occurs in every type of business from universities to small businesses or large corporations and even in personal relationships.

Some people will simply quit and find a new job, but that may not always be an option. Another option that is more readily available is to file a complaint with someone, usually human resources, about a hostile work environment. This option has become more available because of the abundance of sexual harassment issues in the country but has broad enough parameters to cover other harassment situation as well. I wasn't aware of this as an option at the time.

Another option would be to have what I call a "clearing conversation" with the antagonist. During this conversation it is critical to simply address the problem or behavior and not attack the person. To do this, I mentally separate myself as if I am watching a game unfold in an arena before me. I keep emotions out and address the issue at hand. I use phrases such as, "My experience of you is . . ." or, "How I feel around you is . . ." These are self-accountable statements that address how I feel without attacking the other person. The example in the previous pages might have been addressed in the following manner: I could have approached my training officer to talk and used phrases such as, "My experience of you is, it is your way or the highway. Even though there are several ways to solve the problem, I feel if it isn't the one way you want, it will be wrong. Even if it works. How I feel around you is frustrated and lost. I feel stymied and held back."

Notice, there are no personal attacks, and I am self-accountable because it is how I am feeling. Unfortunately, at the time I wasn't aware of this technique and wasn't emotionally prepared to do this.

When things were good, I shared, but when they weren't going well, I bottled up and didn't say anything. I knew my choices were limited so I concentrated on being a good patrol officer in the hopes that something might change. I have always been an optimist, knowing things would turn out fine. During this time, I knew that I would get by, and that is what I did. I got by, and I survived.

The city was extremely quiet one late night on patrol. A heavy overcast sky and off-and-on rain made the night seem darker than normal. Lightning glimmered through the clouds followed by small rumbles of thunder. It was late, and all of the businesses were closed. The streets were empty, giving an eerie feeling of being watched even though no one was around. The night was so slow that my training officer wanted to take time to cover some required paperwork with me. We left our patrol area and headed to the office, driving carefully on the damp roads. Just as we arrived at the office, dispatch called, and of course there was a suspicious person at the McDonald's in my area. I immediately made a U-turn and headed back to my area, slightly frustrated because we had been trying for weeks to get this paperwork done and thought we would finally have time to do it.

I arrived at the McDonald's and parked in a lot at the rear of the store, where we could approach safely and unseen. There were no lights on in the restaurant. which had closed for the night a couple hours earlier. My training officer followed closely behind me while I checked the dented and scraped metal back door of the business. It was secure. I worked my way up the south side of the building, approaching the glass drive-through window and checked. It was closed tight and secure. There was a large lightning flash, parting the clouds with bright light and creating dark shadows from any overhanging trees and power poles. I worked my way up to the south side entrance and tested the doors. They too were shut tight and would only open in the morning with the manager's key. I moved to the front of the building, looking through the large glass windows for anything suspicious inside, moving a little quicker to get to the doors around the corner that opened into the children's play area. I rounded the corner just as a large bolt of lightning split the sky, nearly blinding me, followed immediately by a booming roll of thunder that echoed for seconds. As the light from the lightning lit up the night a large shadowy figure loomed over me moving rapidly.

I jumped out of my skin and yelled stop, as I started to pull my weapon to point at the oncoming threat. Suddenly, I melted and sheepishly lowered my weapon back into my holster. I had almost shot Ronald McDonald. The large plastic statue guarding the children's play area had appeared to move and advance as its shadow moved with the lightning. I was embarrassed but checked the rest of the building and located no suspicious person. I now had a feeling that someone had been driving past during a flash of lightning and that their call was really about a suspicious statue that appeared to move in the blustery, lightning-filled night. My training officer and I both laughed about that encounter as we headed back to the office to catch up on our paperwork that night.

It was nice to have a trainer that could laugh at humorous things and allowed me to be me. Yes, I started to draw my weapon. But I put no one at risk. My trainer told me he saw the shadows from behind me and thought someone was charging and was stepping up to assist.

I shared this with my wife because it was too funny not to, and because I was relieved that I had received a passing score from my trainer that night. I knew from hard previous experience there could have been a different result. I was still lacking trust but that was slowly changing. As things at work got better, I began to open up at home also. We started to talk a little more, and things were heading back into the realms of normality.

CHAPTER 7

IVY AND MORE

S hortly after completing my second field training, I was dispatched to an apartment complex on a domestic disturbance. A guy had pulled a shotgun out and threatened his wife as she was running out the front door. This was reported by the wife who added that he had gone back inside the apartment. We arrived, and two officers went to the front while I was assigned to watch the back. It was a two-story building, with two windows for each apartment on the rear. The suspect's apartment was on the second floor. The officers knocked at the front door, with no response. They yelled into the door and still, no response. The wife had given them the key to the door, and with her permission they entered to search.

Meanwhile, I was out back and approaching the building in case the suspect jumped out the second story window. Thinking about the reported shotgun, I positioned myself behind a large tree with a clear view of the two rear windows belonging to the suspect's apartment. Once the other officers were inside the apartment, they searched. They notified dispatch and me that the apartment was unoccupied. I did not see anything at the rear of the apartment and stepped out from behind the tree to look for any signs of the suspect. A neighbor kid, playing and riding his scooter nearby, yelled over to me. He had seen the suspect jump out of the window earlier. He said, "He's right there." I asked "Where?" and the boy pointed down, near my feet.

I was standing in thick, overgrown ivy vines, about knee deep, and when I looked down where he was pointing, I saw nothing but vines. I looked closer and saw the barely visible tip of the pointed toe of a cowboy boot. It was about two feet to my left. The adrenaline instantly flooded my body as my heart rate went up rapidly. The suspect had a shotgun. I quickly backed away, pulled my weapon from the holster on my right hip and used the large tree as cover. I called out on the radio, and the other officers ran around the building to assist me. We took the suspect into custody at gunpoint. Turned out I had gotten lucky. We learned the suspect had jumped out the rear window as we arrived. When he jumped out the window, his shotgun got caught on the window frame and fell to the floor, behind the couch, under the window he had escaped through. The officers found it there later.

———————

I had someone tell me once, "Sometimes it's better to be lucky than good." In this case I agree with that sentiment. I didn't share any of this experience with my wife. I didn't want her to worry. Instead, I put another brick in the wall. At this point in my marriage, I continued to hold back, choosing not to share many things. When something good would happen, I would share parts of that. If I were to do it over, I would have shared everything. For one thing, it was evident to me that someone or something was watching over me. I never shared how it made me feel in that situation. I felt lucky that the suspect had dropped the weapon, and I felt good that we made the arrest, and no one was hurt. I was a little frightened by what could have happened if he had still been armed and hidden two feet from me. I was grateful for the kid who pointed the suspect out so I could live another day. For any family or friend relationship to flourish, it is imperative that we communicate and include them in our lives, especially our spouses. We may not be able to share details of events, but it is extremely important that we share how we felt about the events and how they affected us emotionally.

During this time, things went well at work other than a few comments from my early detractors which were easily blown off by my actions and the way I did my job. I was again the idealistic rookie in this phase of my career. I had been knocked down hard but had gotten back up and was still in the fight. Now, I started to see the hard parts of life as we dealt daily with "bad people, or good people having a really bad day." I was in the up-and-down phase, emotionally, as I would get excited to go on a hot call. I would feel good about the way I handled it, and then one of my detractors would bring it up in roll call and intimate that I should have done it a different way or had done something wrong. At the time it played with my mind and my confidence, and that is just what they wanted as certain groups of officers still didn't and never would accept that I was a solo officer. In hindsight, I should have gone to another department and gotten myself into a better situation, but I was overly loyal to those who hired me and felt I owed them something.

Meanwhile, this rollercoaster affected my relationships at home. When I was criticized at work, I let it eat at me. My ego would replay it over and over. I would let it bother me and then would be short tempered at home with my wife and kids. I still worked and made decisions around the house, but I was starting to withdraw from being around some people. I had not wanted to let law enforcement become my life, but it was what I thought about most of the time.

I learned how to be tough and suck it up as a young man, and that is what I did in this situation. I held it in and put on a brave face. No one would know I was bothered. Unfortunately, I did not know how to open up to those who cared without opening up to everyone. To be safe, I sucked it up, held it in, and opened up to no one.

———————

One Labor Day weekend, after becoming a solo officer, I came into work on Monday morning. As I pulled into the parking lot, I saw a car, a lowrider Nissan or Toyota, parked in what was then the detective's parking area. It was not parked normally and took up two parking places in the tiny parking lot, making it hard for officers to find a parking place before going into briefing. What stood out, in addition to the bad parking job, was blood dripping from the driver's side rear door onto the asphalt below. We learned the driver had committed suicide with a handgun on the previous Friday evening. Since it was a holiday weekend, there was no place to take the car as everything was closed. The responding detective had the car towed to the department parking space, thus explaining the bad parking job. During the weekend, temperatures had risen, and it was quite warm. The heat created problems with the pool of blood on the floorboards behind the driver's seat. The stench was overpowering, and flies were starting to gather. The smell and the sight of blood dripping from the car is memorable to this day. I know that smell stuck with me for a long time.

At the time, I didn't think this had stuck with me, but the fact that I remember it so clearly, to this day, proves that idea wrong. I have seen much worse, but this is still one of my memories. This is a great example of how trauma creeps up on us. Some things that we think don't really matter, or laugh off as if they are nothing, stay hidden in the shadows of our mind, lurking in dark corners. They often poison our emotional wellbeing for years, and we are not aware of it. We insist it was nothing and that we are strong and have moved past it. Then in the future, something triggers that memory. That is when we learn that we can only work through it by confronting these memories, bringing them out into the light, and admitting the fear or distress the event caused. We can change the paradigm of our life by sharing these things with friends and family and even therapists. Then the negative power of these events are removed.

CHAPTER 8

THE RIGHT PLACE AT THE RIGHT TIME

I had been in patrol as a solo officer for about a year when an interesting string of events occurred in the span of one week. The first was a Tuesday morning, when a car was stolen from the student parking lot at what was then Jordan High School. At that time there was a lot of empty, undeveloped land within the city. Jordan High School was bordered on the west by State Street, and there were empty fields to the south of the school. The stolen car was reported by a witness as last seen going south on State Street. Patrol officers coming up State Street from the south did not see the car. There was only one place for it to be: in the large area of fields and undeveloped land, just south of the school. This area was huge, with rolling hills, covered with high brush, clumps of scrub oak, and large gnarly cottonwood trees along a canal bank that cut across the middle of the property. It was big enough that a person could not see across the property with the naked eye. It was part of my patrol area, so I took charge and coordinated a containment of the area to be searched. All four sides of the area were covered, and a two-man team was sent in to the field to search. They were the best search team we could have asked for. One K9 officer, his large German Shepherd, and a second officer were there to back them up. About half an hour into the search, the stolen car was located, abandoned in an overgrown field near the canal. And now the fun began. An officer was assigned to watch the car, in case the suspect returned to it, and the K9 search team was let loose. The K9 began his track at the car and was hot on the trail, nose to the ground, moving steadily forward. As the suspect's scent got stronger, the dog began to bark. A short time into the search, the dog stopped at the top of the canal bank, next to a large cottonwood tree and started barking ferociously at the tree. It took a while as officers searched. Nothing was visible in or around the tree. There was no indication or evidence of the suspect's presence. The dog, lunging on his lead, still barked aggressively at the tree and would not give up. Because of the K9's insistence, officers continued to search the area around the tree and located the suspect. He was on the canal bank, covered in mud, burrowed underneath the roots of the tree that hung into the water, in a muddy hole. One of the captains of the department had joined me as I had coordinated the search. When the call was complete and the suspect in custody, he told me, "Good job. It was nice to just watch and not have to take over."

Four days later, on Saturday morning about 0630 hours (6:30 a.m.) a call came in of a residential burglary in progress. The call wasn't in my area, but I was nearby and was familiar with the area. I knew there were only three ways into that subdivision. I took the nearest way and called out on the radio to other officers who were approaching and told them I was at the north entrance, then told them to cover the west and south streets that came into that area. I got lucky as I was driving into the area on that north street. The suspect vehicle was described as a beat-up red Subaru, and here it came approaching me down the street. When it passed by me, I made a U-turn to go after him, and the chase began. The first street we turned onto was a U-shaped street, lined with parked cars on both sides. It was narrow. I probably had a foot clearance on each side of my car as I flew up the street, siren screaming. It was also the street that my new chief of police lived on. We got through that street, and the suspect turned right, heading north. I continued to follow, close on his tail. The suspect then turned right again, heading east toward Big Cottonwood Canyon, where Alta and Snowbird Ski Resorts are located. There was very little traffic this early in the morning, which was good. We were traveling fast and soon exited the city and entered the canyon. As one travels east up the canyon, the ski resorts are on the right hand, downhill side of the road. The uphill, left-hand side of the road is covered with pine and aspen trees, brush, and rocks. The suspect continued east, past Snowbird Ski Resort, traveling on the windy canyon roads at high speed, continually looking back at the red and blue flashing lights behind him. Without warning, he suddenly veered left onto a barely visible dirt road. I was right on his bumper. The dirt from the road flew into the air, filling it with thick dust and making it difficult to see. The road stopped in the middle of the forest about a quarter mile later, and the suspect, a white male in his mid-twenties, jumped out of the car and ran, crashing down the mountain dodging trees and rocks. He weaved back and forth and side to side, looking like a star halfback avoiding defenders on a game-winning run with time running out in the game. Being the bulldog I was, and already in chase mode, I stayed close on his tail. We plunged downhill a couple hundred yards, through the shiny white aspens and bushy branched pines, and crossed the main paved road we had just left. Then we scrambled, like mountain goats, bounding from rock to rock, down a steep hundred-foot retaining embankment covered with rocks as large as a Volkswagen Beetle. We plunged into the parking area of the Alta Ski Resort Lodge. He ran around the side of the lodge to a rear parking area. I was about fifteen yards behind him. He kept looking back with frightened, drug-crazed eyes as we ran, not believing I was still there. When I rounded the corner of the lodge, he was gone, vanished like a wisp of smoke caught in a breeze. I knew he had not gone into the woods beyond the parking lot because I would have seen him crossing the parking lot. The large beat-up metal delivery doors on the back of the lodge had mechanisms to slowly close, and they were still shut tight, so I knew he had not gone into any of them. There were five or six cars in the parking lot, so I started searching around them and found the suspect hiding under one of the cars. At least his head and shoulders were under the car. He was like a three-year-old child playing hide and seek, thinking, "If I can't see you then you can't see me." His body sticking out from under one of the cars was a dead giveaway. I cautiously approached, ordered and pulled him from under the car, and put the cuffs on him. He offered no resistance as he breathed heavily from the exertion we had just gone through. Then, I realized I was going to have a long rugged uphill hike, with him in tow, to get to my car. I couldn't call on my radio for assistance, because at that time our radios/walkies did not work in the mountains. We didn't have cell phones. Now what? I felt a throbbing in my knee and felt blood oozing down my leg. I realized I had cut my knee going down the rocky embankment. It later required stitches. What I did not know was that the Alta town marshal was in his office, on the mountain above the resort. When he heard my siren coming up the canyon, he started watching through binoculars and was on the landline with dispatch, keeping them up to date on what was happening and where I was. Thus, as I stood there contemplating my next move and slowly began to start the long, rugged, uphill walk with my prisoner, here came the marshal. Then a couple of patrol cars from my shift arrived, and finally a medical unit, who patched up my knee until I could get to the hospital and get stitched up. When I got done at the hospital, my sergeant told me I could take the rest of the day off. I was so pumped up on adrenaline, I couldn't, so I changed my torn pants, polished my rock-scraped boots, and worked on my report. It was really nice, as I sat there in the office writing my report, when officers and office staff would come by to congratulate me on a job well done.

Three days later, on another Tuesday, I was working the south sector of the city. At about 1100 hours (11:00 a.m.) a call of a serious hit-and-run accident with injuries in the north part of the city was dispatched over our car radios. Officers quickly responded, but the suspect vehicle with two occupants had sped away before they arrived. The officers stopped to assist the seriously injured victims. A description of the suspect vehicle was also broadcast and was reported as leaving the scene of the accident northbound, out of the city. I was walking into a restaurant in my area at 1130 hours (11:30 a.m.) with two other officers when I had a firm feeling in my gut about that car. It strongly prompted me to go out to the nearby intersection. I actually listened to that feeling and told the guys I would be right back. I drove out of the restaurant parking lot as it was quickly filling with patrons, turned right (north) onto the roadway and stopped at a red stoplight at the intersection, a couple hundred feet later. As I sat at the light, I looked to the left, and there was the hit-and-run suspect vehicle with two occupants driving east, making a left turn to go north, in front of me. As they turned left in front of me, I called out on the radio and turned on my overhead lights and went after them. They stopped about a block north of the intersections. There were tall fences on both sides of the road, and I was praying the two occupants wouldn't run, because I still had stitches in my knee from earlier in the week. Since the accident was a serious hit-and-run accident with critical injuries, and I had multiple suspects in the car, I was very careful as I approached. Backup officers quickly arrived. They turned out to be the chief of police, and the lieutenant over detectives. Once the suspects were in custody and being transported to the office for questioning, the chief turned and said to me, "You sure seem to be in the right place at the right time, lately." Three weeks later, I was surprised by being assigned to Detectives, where I worked for the next eight years.

———————

During this time, I opened up a little. At home, I talked and worked with my wife, raised the kids, and took care of the house. I shared a lot of what happened at work. Fortunately, there were no calls that I would consider extremely threatening. My wife still had problems with depression, but we worked through that the best we could, considering we did not know anything about it. I remembered the relationship advice from the academy to develop hobbies outside of law enforcement and chose to continue teaching scuba diving as my non-work-related activity. I was very good at it. I taught scuba diving two evenings a week, and every other week I spent my days off camping with my family at the lake where I conducted the open water training for the scuba courses. My wife had become a divemaster and enjoyed helping me teach. We all loved diving and camping out at the lake. Those couple of years passed quickly. I was in tune with life, open, communicating, and things were going well in every aspect of life. Work was good as I handled new calls and gained experience as an officer and then as a detective. The criticism at work had decreased, in part because I avoided, to the best of my ability, working shifts with people I did not trust. There was still an underlying current of negative feelings, but I chose not to let that affect me. This current continued as there was some resentment from older officers toward me for making detective so quickly. During this time, I tested for sergeant the first time. I didn't make the top five, but I told myself it was my first experience and there would be other chances.

CHAPTER 9

THE NEW DETECTIVE

Being a detective was an interesting experience and looking back I realize it wasn't a good fit at that time. More experience as a patrol officer would have been beneficial. It was not necessarily the job I was ill prepared for. It was mostly the management style and dealing with a different kind of politics that got me. I was there for eight years. These were years in which I learned a great deal, but for the most part they weren't fun years.

My sergeant was very old school and relished having the reputation of being a hardcase. He never offered a good or positive word. When he pointed out a mistake or error, it was very harsh and intimidating. He would give everyone a good enough evaluation to get a raise but rarely high enough or low enough to cause him extra paperwork to justify that evaluation. There was no mentoring or, in my opinion now, true leadership. Many years later I figured out that to get him to leave me alone would have required me standing up to him, but at that time I didn't see that as a possibility. Everyone just said, "That's just his way." It appeared later that he was unhappy because of problems in his personal life. His wife was quite ill with a terminal disease. These issues seemed to dictate his moods, which were usually bad or worse. At the time I did not understand that he was gruff and ornery because he did not want to be close to anyone and was hurting. He was dealing with serious issues at home, and his behavior wasn't really about me or anyone else. It was about protecting himself from being hurt more. Now I know it wasn't all about me; a lot of it was about him, and I can give him the benefit of the doubt. I have learned now that I can care and withstand these types of situations by being self-accountable, communicating openly and honestly, and without giving away my own integrity.

———————

The situation with my sergeant went on for the entire eight years I was a detective, plus a few years afterward. In some ways this reminded me of growing up with my father. My father was much more positive but always pointed out what I did wrong, so (in his mind) I could fix it and be better. One incident stands out in my mind. When I was twelve years old, I was a catcher on my baseball team. I played in a game and had the game of my life. I was not a great hitter, but I hit three for five that night. I caught a foul tip as I climbed the screen of the backstop, and even though the pitcher was really erratic and wild that night, I stopped all balls from getting past me. Everything went as well as it could, except that three guys stole second base, and my throws to second were not accurate. When my throw to second was off, the runner at third base would come home and score. The next day while working in the back yard doing chores, my dad approached. He had a five-gallon bucket full of baseballs and our baseball mitts. He told me, "Your throws to second last night were terrible. Let's go work on them." He took me to the ballpark and emptied the bucket of balls onto the pitcher's mound. He then placed the bucket at second base with the open-end facing home plate. He would pitch the ball to me at home plate, in my catcher's position, and I was to throw the ball into the bucket. If the ball missed the bucket, it would roll to the outfield fence, 320 feet away. When we were out of baseballs, I would pick up the empty bucket and run around the outfield, picking up the balls. Then we would do it again. I remember how hot it was in the middle of June in the ninety-degree heat of summer. He never told me how good I did the night before, even having the game of my life. He never told me what I did well. He only told me what I did wrong. In this aspect, he and my sergeant were a lot alike. This may be one reason I was so uncomfortable around my sergeant and could have contributed to why I never spoke up or said anything. On the other hand, my sergeant had his current problems in life, in addition to the things in his past that were influencing the way he responded. How was his relationship with his father? His mother? How was he treated as a child? We don't know any of these things, and as I get older, I have learned that everyone has a story. Some sort of trauma in their life. If we could see every detail in a person's past, in their present, and into their heart and mind, I am sure we would react to a given situation in a far different manner.

CHURCH ARSON

In one of my first cases as a new detective, a young man in his early twenties decided he did not like the Church of Jesus Christ of Latter-day Saints (the Mormon church). To show this, he chose to break into one of the local ward houses (a local church). He collected nearby chairs, rugs, random books, and whatever other miscellaneous items he could find from around the building. He piled them together in the chapel in the same pattern Boy Scouts use when preparing a campfire. Then he lit them on fire. Fortunately, he did not use any type of accelerant, and the fire slowly burned itself out before it got out of control. Other than smoke, there was relatively little damage. I canvassed the neighborhood thoroughly, giving special focus to the neighbors near the church, and got some useful information. I followed up on those leads and discovered that a possible suspect lived in the neighborhood. There was a lot of third-hand information including someone saying something to someone, who told the bishop, who called me. The young man in question had been disciplined by his parents and the church and was angry about it. He was angry at the church for siding with his parents. The information the bishop told me verified information I had discovered when speaking with neighbors and looking at the crime scene. I interviewed the young man. He confessed, and the case was solved. The local news wanted the story because arson of a Mormon church is a big deal, especially in the heart of Salt Lake City, the home of the Mormon church's headquarters. The chief gave me permission to talk to the news. I was excited. When I got home, I told my wife that I was going to be on the news that night. The news story was positive toward police, but while watching, all I could think and say was, "That's not what I said," or, "That's not what happened." The real story seemed rather mundane to me, but the reporters had edited it to make it more sensational. That was when I realized that the news is all about marketing and sales and generally won't let the truth get in the way of a good story. I was disappointed and didn't watch the news for several years after that and am still extremely skeptical when I watch.

FREQUENT FLYERS

There was another young man who was a constant problem in our community and for the police. He came from an upper middle-class family and lived in the country club area of town. He was involved in assaults, thefts, drugs, and about anything else you can think of, but he always got away with it. Somehow, someone would change their story, or someone else would end up taking the blame. His parents, especially his mother, covered up for him. On one occasion, officers chased him from a nearby crime scene on foot and finally caught and tackled him in the front yard of his home. Suddenly a speeding car came flying off the street, over the curb, and into the yard. The car slid to a stop, leaving deep tire marks, tearing up sod, and nearly hitting the officers as they were placing him in custody. It was the young man's mother, like an angry lioness, coming to protect her cub. That was typical of the crazy, unpredictable behavior demonstrated by this family.

At one point, the parents of one of this young man's friends were out of town, so the kids decided to have a small party of friends that turned into a large, overcrowded mixture of friends, acquaintances, and even strangers. When the parents returned a few days later, they noticed things missing from the house including jewelry, antique firearms and swords, and most notably a $10,000 diamond cocktail ring. Rumor said that this young man was involved.

I was assigned the case and started visiting antique dealers and pawn shops. At one local pawn shop I found all of the jewelry, except the expensive cocktail ring. The suspect's girlfriend had pawned them. I had her now, but I knew she wouldn't turn him in. It also did not make sense that every piece of jewelry was there but one. I went back a couple days later to double check. A different employee of the pawn shop told me he remembered that ring. He thought it was in the safe in the owner's office. It was late on a Friday, and he let me know the owner would not be back until Monday. I went back on Monday and met the owner for the second time. He admitted that the ring had been there but claimed he sold it to a good customer a few days before. He refused to give the customer's name, and at that time, the laws were written in such a way that I could not pursue it successfully. I'm sure he sold it to family or a friend but will never know for sure.

The girlfriend taking these items to the pawn shop was the link to my suspect. In my interview with her, she let slip about a small antique store that I did not know about. I went there and met the owner, a retired marine, who was a great guy. Two of the stolen antique swords and an antique rifle had been sold to him. Fortunately, he had photocopied the seller's ID, and it was my suspect. This was the proof I was looking for.

There was still a lot of other property missing, so with this new evidence I got a search warrant for the suspect's home. When we got there, we found that the entire basement of the 3500-square-foot home had been taken over by the eighteen-year-old suspect. I found several rifles and shotguns under his bed. They had all been reported stolen in different burglaries. These and other stolen items located throughout the basement connected him to at least four other residential burglaries. We also found a large amount of marijuana, hidden in the sauna. He went to trial and was convicted on several felony charges, and for the first time he went to prison. His overly protective mother of course claimed we had planted everything.

It seems things haven't changed much over the years, since this is just one example of the judgment heaped on law enforcement then and today. If someone can't get off on the merits of the case, blame the officer. Officers deal with this type of thing on a daily basis, and it is just another added stress in our lives. Even when the claims are untrue and unfounded, many have to go through an internal investigation, which is still another stress. Social media today has made it even worse as officers are now tried and judged before the facts are even known. It is sad how many officers' careers are ruined in the media and social media blitz after an event, only to be exonerated weeks or months later after a full investigation when all of the facts are known. Unfortunately, their career is still over.

CHAPTER 10

MAGICAL MYSTERY TOUR

When I started in Detectives, I was assigned to work juvenile cases, which I enjoyed greatly. There were no officers from our department in any of the schools at the time, so I handled the whole city and anything juvenile related. I decided it would be a good idea to go out on Friday and Saturday nights to work the streets and take all calls that were juvenile related, especially any kid parties. My purpose was twofold: First, if I took the calls it would free up a patrol unit to handle other calls. Second, the kids who were out causing problems on the weekends were the kids I would be dealing with as I handled juvenile crime. I would start work between 1600 and 2000 hours (4:00-8:00 p.m.) and work an eight-hour shift. One Friday night, it finally quieted down, and I started heading home at about 0300 (3:00 a.m.). Some of the guys were going to a twenty-four-hour restaurant for breakfast and invited me. I didn't have any extra money, and since my home was only fifteen minutes away, I told them, "Thanks, but I am heading home."

I left the restaurant parking lot heading east toward home. I am diabetic and as I drove away from the restaurant my blood sugar dropped so low that I lost consciousness. I came to in the pitch dark and had no idea where I was or how long I had been there. I knew I was in the mountains but could not see anything around me. My car was running, but my headlights shined off into a dark void. I couldn't see anything but the pinpoint gleam of a small campfire on what appeared to be a mountainside several miles away toward my right-hand side. All I could figure out was that I was up high, in the mountains, somewhere.

I called out on my car radio for help, and no one answered. I called out again, and still no answer. Our radios still did not work up in the mountains, away from the city. I sat there for what seemed like forever, thinking, trying in my clouded brain to solve the question of where I was and what I could do about it. I looked around, trying to see anything that would give me a hint of where I was or how I could get help. I looked over at my passenger seat, and a vague thought formed in my foggy brain. I saw my new brick cell phone that I had recently been issued. I was barely able to pick it up and dial 911, but I did, and suddenly I was talking to someone. It was the dispatch center in Salt Lake City, the largest city in the area, about fifteen miles north of Sandy City. I explained that I was Detective Williams and was diabetic and having an insulin reaction. I did not know where I was and needed help.

A massive multi-county search was initiated. I learned later that Summit County sheriffs were searching the mountains on the Park City side, the east side of the Wasatch Mountains. Salt Lake County and several other agencies were searching the canyons on the Salt Lake side, west side of the Wasatch Mountains. The Tooele County sheriffs were searching the Oquirrh Mountains on the west side of the Salt Lake Valley. They also contacted my wife to make sure I was not at home.

Dispatch told me to activate all of my lights, so I lowered the sun visor of my unmarked detective car and turned on the red and blue flashers. I then turned on all of the lights to my car and put the headlights to bright as they flashed on and off.

Finally, about 0500 (5:00 a.m.), the dark began to subside as light from the barely rising sun peeked over the top of the mountain. The sky lightened up just enough. I could now see a little bit. The sun was rising behind me, and I was on a mountain top. Just off to my left, barely visible in the predawn light, I could see the dark shadowy image of a ski lift tower. When I told that to dispatch, they narrowed down the search area to two canyons. About half an hour later, a fire truck slowly pulled up behind me on the rough terrain. A Sandy Police car followed along behind, obscured by the dust rising from the narrow dirt path. The officers walked up, peered through my open driver's side window, and saw that my car was in drive. I was sitting there with both feet pressed firmly onto the brake pedal. They asked me to put my car into park, and in a slow, uncoordinated manner, I did. Apparently, I had driven twelve miles up the curving road of Big Cottonwood Canyon and past Snowbird Ski Resort and Alta Ski Resort. Someone had left the gate to the service road open, and I had driven up the narrow, winding, dirt service road. I was now sitting near the top ski lift tower of Alta. If I had driven another fifty feet, my car would have been hurtling down the steep, upper ski runs of the resort. It is amazing that there was no damage to my car anywhere. I drove twelve miles up a curvy canyon road with steep drop offs along some of the curves, through a narrow gate, onto a narrow, winding, dirt road, through boulders and trees, in the pitch dark, and didn't hit anything or drive off the road over steep, rocky drop-offs. I am still amazed at that. The Salt Lake City Dispatch Center sent me a first aid kit filled with candy and told me to make sure I didn't scare them like that, ever again. The guys at work, especially my sergeant, called this my Magical Mystery Tour and had fun at my expense. I deserved it. I learned after I retired that this incident was brought up repeatedly by one captain and was used to keep me from getting promoted thirteen times over the next seventeen years.

This experience scared me, as well as my wife. It was one more thing to stress about. I started carrying candy or something sweet with me, especially at night when many stores were closed. This was still in the early phase of my time in Detectives, and I was still open and talking. I especially had to be open in this case to solve the issue and not put my life or anyone else's in jeopardy ever again.

When my second daughter was in junior high school and was learning about the Oregon Trail and the pioneers who traveled it, she wanted to visit and see the trail. The Oregon Trail ran near my parent's hometown in Nebraska. I had visited that spot several times, but it was an eight-hour drive away. I researched and found part of the trail in Idaho, only a three-hour drive away. We set off one Saturday to go take pictures and gather information for her school report.

We got to Idaho and found the area. It was in the middle of nowhere. There was nothing around for miles, and there was snow on the ground. The weather changed quickly, and the icy wind shifted as it blew in from the north. Before long, it started to snow. We drove off the highway and onto a narrow dirt road. After a short drive, we found the spot and could barely see the wagon ruts under the snow. We took a few pictures and were so cold we decided we could relate to why the pioneers did not travel this trail in the winter.

We started to turn the car around to leave for home when the snow crunched under the passenger side of the car. Suddenly that side of the car dropped, and we were leaning to one side, stuck in the snow. I knew we were in trouble because we were off the main roads and no one knew exactly where we were. It was getting darker and colder. I had nothing to work with to get us out. I looked around and found a piece of wood from a broken fence line. After a couple of hours of using that stray piece of board, digging, struggling, pushing and rocking the car, I finally broke the car loose and got us out. We slowly drove home in the slick, icy storm. I gradually warmed my frozen hands and feet on the drive. My daughter got an A on her report, and she learned about the Oregon Trail history, experiencing it in a way most people today won't. We still talk about this experience today and laugh a little about it. I didn't tell her how scared I was until years later. I was not prepared, and we both learned from that. Now we both keep a sleeping bag, shovel, and other necessities in the car, especially in the winter.

This incident was a close call and showed how unprepared I was. It taught me and my daughter a real-life lesson about being prepared, in the physical sense. I handled physical stress fine, but there was also the other side of the coin, the emotional side of my life, in which I was equally unprepared. I've since learned it is just as important that we learn how to handle stressful situations in a way that we can still live full, effective, productive, and happy lives, rather than just survive. I did not know enough about communication to say what I wanted effectively, and I was fearful of saying the wrong thing, so I held back and didn't say anything. My history shows how well that worked.

What are some things we can do to foster healthy communication? We can speak directly, openly, and honestly, addressing the problem instead of attacking the person. As far as dealing with stress, there are many ways to reduce stress and what works depends on the person. Some general options include the following:

1. Physical exercise. I started running and rode my bicycle. I actually had one marriage counselor tell my wife that if she wanted to talk with me, she needed to go run or ride with me.

For some reason, I opened up and communicated better when I was physically active.

2. Meditation. This can be as simple as breathing exercises—a technique similar to combat breathing that we learn in law enforcement. Yoga is another option for meditative exercise and is quite effective. One thing I found that was new and different and works well is Tibetan bowls or singing bowls. The harmony and vibrations can put one into a meditative state. Some of these techniques are outside the wheelhouse of many law enforcement officers, but if what we are doing is not working, then it is time to look outside the box and find something that does work. There are many other options that are listed toward the end of this book.

CHAPTER 11

CLOSING OFF

One day I went home for lunch. As I drove out of my subdivision, heading back to the office, I stopped at a red light. A car containing what looked like four or five gang members, wearing bandanas and proudly flying their colors, approached the intersection from the left, then turned left at the light heading away from me. This car drew my attention as it was unusual for that area. Four or five minority guys in a beat-up (POS) older car flying gang colors and wearing matching bandanas and shirts. The color of the day was red. Something told me to follow them. I was on my way to a mandatory weekly Detective meeting and had a choice. My sergeant was gruff and not a pleasure to work for, especially when he was unhappy with me. If I followed the car, I would be late, my sergeant would be angry, and I would become the target of the day or week. I chose to ignore the feeling and go to the meeting. At the meeting a vehicle description and suspect information was given for some armed robbery suspects, and yes, it was the guys I had just seen and not followed.

I had a feeling I should follow those guys but shut down my feelings so much that I made conscious choices to ignore them. This behavior carried over into my personal relationships with my wife, since I rarely talked anymore. I was stressed at work again and quit talking about work. Even worse, I did not share how I felt about anything. Subconsciously, I was protecting myself. Realistically, I was destroying the one thing I cared about most: my marriage. The wall was getting bigger and stronger. These are choices I made, which eventually ended the relationship, giving it no chance to be repaired.

NAVY SEAL/BEANIE BOY?

One day I was out in a neighborhood, following up on some leads in a case, when I was approached by a guy. He said, "Hey, I just got home from the Navy, and I've got to get my niece and her friends out of my house." I started to explain that it sounded like a civil issue when he interrupted me and said, "No, they have been cooking meth, and if you will work with me, I can get you their lab. It's taken down right now, but I will help you get it and them." Then he went on to tell me he used to do this kind of thing in the Navy in South America, because he was a SEAL. He said he could take them down himself but did not want to hurt anyone.

I looked at him and thought, *no way are you a SEAL*. He was about 5'6" to 5'7", a little on the chubby side, and did not have the mannerisms or physical movements of a warrior. He came to the office a few days later to give me information, dressed in his dark blue Navy uniform. He had on a medal that covered half his chest. Later I learned it looked like the Navy SEAL Special Warfare badge, also known as the SEAL Trident or Budweiser. I say *looked like*, because there was no way this guy was a

SEAL. A few days later, he returned to the office. Again, he was in his blue uniform, looking sharp. But this time he had added to his uniform. In addition to his oversized badge, he was wearing a multicolored beanie with a propeller on top.

He told me the suspects were finally moving and disposing of the lab. It was in parts, and some of the pieces were in a garbage can in front of the house, waiting to be picked up for disposal. Since it was in an area accessible to the public and open, I did not need a warrant. I checked, and sure enough there was glassware, tubing, and other components for a meth lab, minus the chemicals. I made arrangements with the waste disposal company to send an empty truck to pick up that trash can only and recovered the evidence without having to climb through garbage. The equipment tested positive for meth, and I was able to arrest the suspects. To this day, I am sure this guy was not a SEAL, and I'm not sure he was even in the Navy. Some of the other detectives made fun of me and made fun of "Beanie Boy," but that stopped when his information was good, and we took down a lab and got two felony convictions for manufacturing meth.

This was a fun case to work, but it showed the deceptions officers deal with, even from those who may be working to help us but in reality, are using us to solve a problem they have.

Later in life I realized that everyone, myself included, wears masks to protect ourselves. I was tough at work, never asking for help, even when I could have used it. I appeared arrogant to keep people away. I never opened up to my sergeant, even knowing it would have made life easier. I just withdrew and worked as hard as I could, avoiding the problem. That was my escape then. Now, I am wide open and hide nothing. I let people know what I am thinking, and life is so much simpler. Communication is key, and now I communicate simply. I know that the story is just that, a story. Get rid of the drama and say what you mean, openly and honestly. It makes life a lot easier.

HIGH ROLLER

At one point I had a fraudulent check case where the suspect was stealing checks and forging them. He had already cashed or purchased several thousand dollars of merchandise. He put on the image of being very wealthy and dressed in fashionable, high-end clothes. As I was following the trail of forged checks in my attempt to locate him, I found that he had purchased a used black Jaguar in a neighboring city. He had given them $2000 in cash and had written a check for the remaining $33,000. Of course, the cash was obtained with a stolen check, and the check for the balance was also stolen and forged.

During my investigation, I noticed a pattern. There was a credit union service center in my city that provided services for every credit union in the area. A lot of the checks were being cashed there. There were so many, I suspected there might be a service center employee involved. I spoke with the manager and employees and ruled that out. They did recognize the suspect from his frequent visits. I gave them my direct phone number, (yes, we finally had cell phones) to call me when the suspect came back. They were more than happy and a little excited to do this, as the credit union had lost a lot of money.

A few days later, the manager called and told me the suspect had just walked in. The police department was only a few blocks from the service center, but the only person available to back me up was my sergeant. He agreed and we approached the service center, and I saw the black Jaguar parked at the curb. We were approaching on foot when the suspect exited the building, heading to "his" car. We stopped him on the sidewalk before he could get into the car and arrested him. The suspect was charged with a multitude of crimes including several counts of third-degree felony fraudulent checks, forgery, theft by deception, and a second-degree felony auto theft charge. The car dealership was happy to get the Jaguar back with no damage. The credit union employees were entertained as they watched the arrest and were excited to have participated. I was happy to complete that case, even though my sergeant was not happy because of the paperwork he would have to do. He paid me back by criticizing the way I handled the case.

HOME INVASION COUSINS

I was assigned a case investigating two cousins whose families were well known to police for assaults, thefts, and doing drugs. The two cousins worked together dealing meth and doing armed home invasion robberies. I spent hours each day tracking these guys for a couple of weeks and could not catch up to them. I followed along in their wake, following the debris trail they left in the lives they touched. During this time, I found out that a detective from a neighboring jurisdiction was also chasing them and was having the same problems. We teamed up and started really chasing these guys. We would work our other cases during the day and track the cousins at night. Unfortunately, the cousins were on meth and didn't sleep for days at a time. We were so close on their tails that they couldn't do anything without us catching them. After about four days of working day and night, we were exhausted and needed to get some sleep. But of course, the cousins never slept. They would strike on that night with another robbery.

One night the other detective got a tip that one of the cousins was at his grandmother's apartment. The suspect had participated in several armed home invasion robberies, making this a high-risk venture, so we utilized the SWAT team. A warrant was obtained, and the property was surrounded. The SWAT team went in and thoroughly searched the apartment. A little while later, the team leader came out and called, "Clear." We then went in and ascertained that the suspect was not there, and the information we had received appeared not to be accurate.

The SWAT team and all participants in the operation, except a couple of guys left behind at the front door of the apartment, gathered out front in the parking lot. As we discussed our next move, the other detective called his informant. The informant asked, "Did you look behind the dryer?"

The SWAT team leader took a couple of guys and stormed back into the apartment. He pulled the clothes dryer away from the wall. Behind the dryer, the sheetrock had been cut out. The suspect had slid into the opening and stood up between the walls of the washroom and the bedroom next to it. The dryer had been pushed back in place, hiding the knee-high opening in the wall. The suspect had been there the entire time. Once the containment was pulled and we had moved out front, the suspect slid out of his hole, pushed the dryer back in place, and crawled out a back window and escaped. Some of the SWAT team stayed in the apartment to verify that the suspect was not there. They looked for openings in other walls and punched some holes in walls in suspicious areas, making sure he really was gone.

Because of the disturbance and the presence of the police, the apartment manager evicted Grandma. This really angered her family. They were angry at the cousin who had put Grandma in this position. With information from family members, this cousin was apprehended about a week later.

I soon received information that the other cousin would be in a city on the west side of the valley. Distantly related family members had rural property there, which was wide open, bordering on the mountains with open fields and woods. I approached the area to start my search for the suspect and stopped at a stop sign on a busy road. Then I heard sirens and saw flashing red and blue lights approaching from my right. I waited and saw a yellow Ford pickup truck approaching at high speed, with a sheriff's deputy hot on his tail, lights flashing and siren wailing. The pickup was stolen, and as it passed, I saw the driver.

It was the cousin, my suspect. I quickly turned on my lights and siren, jumped in behind the deputy, and went along to assist if needed. The chase continued on the main street of the small town then out into the country again. The truck gained a small lead but could not outrun the sheriff's helicopter, flying overhead. As we rounded a slight bend the truck was visible off the road in an open field, next to a canal. The driver scrambled down the deep, muddy canal bank, up the other side, and sprinted into an open field. He started running across the field, glancing over his shoulder at us. The trees on the opposite side of the open field were the beginning of the suspect's family's property. If he got there, he would likely escape. As we pondered what to do, we heard a loud clattering noise overhead. The sheriff's helicopter swooped down from above and behind us, then caught up with and hovered over the rapidly sprinting suspect. The powerful rotor blast from the rotating chopper blades created a windstorm of dust and debris, knocking the suspect to the ground. The dust storm was so thick we couldn't see what was happening as the chopper hovered a few feet off the ground. We saw someone jump out of the chopper and disappear into the dust storm on the ground below. A few seconds later, the chopper slid sideways through the air and landed a couple hundred yards away from the suspect, who was now prone on the ground. As the helicopter rotors slowed to a stop, the air and dust cleared. We could now see that the suspect was in handcuffs. One more in custody, and that crime spree was stopped.

This was a big and difficult case for me. I spent hours and hours investigating and chasing, and finally both suspects were convicted and went to prison. I felt then, and still feel today, that I did a good job. Nothing was ever said by my sergeant even though the case was big enough, or maybe just dramatic enough, to make the news on both the night we raided Grandma's apartment and the night we took this cousin into custody.

Around this time, my wife cut back work from full time to part time, which meant I had to find another part-time job to make up for that reduction in income. The timing couldn't have been worse, since we had just added on to the house. My wife started a new part time job, working from home. My oldest daughter was in junior high and wanted to be on the swim team. My wife would not pick her up or take her to practice, because she said it was too far to drive, even though it was only a mile away. Her depression was really kicking into high gear.

I arranged for my daughter to go to a school near the pool. Now all I had to do was take her to school in the morning on my way to work, and she could walk across the parking lot to swim practice after school. I could pick her up after practice. If I was going to be late, there were tables by the facility office where she could do homework until I got there.

My wife crawled into bed in a dark room, and never came out. Eventually she quit even her part-time job, leaving me to work three jobs, sixteen to twenty hours a day, taking care of the kids as I struggled to keep our household afloat. I couldn't even get her to come out for dinner with the family without a fight. I became bitter and resentful. The wall I had started building was complete and solid as feelings of frustration, anger, self-pity, and exhaustion washed over, in, and around every fiber of my being.

My day started at 0600 (6:00 a.m.), getting the kids up for breakfast and school then going to work. Thank goodness my daughters pitched in. I would come back and take the oldest to junior high while the younger two kids would walk with neighbors to their elementary school. I worked at the police department until around 1700 hours (5:00 p.m.) and would pick my oldest daughter up from swimming, go home, and make a quick dinner for the kids. I would assign dishes and laundry chores to the kids, then go to a part-time job. On Mondays and Wednesdays, I would teach scuba diving from 1830 (6:30 p.m.) to 2300 (11:00 p.m.) then stop at the grocery store on the way home to get things for the next couple days of dinners. On Tuesdays, Thursdays, Fridays, and Saturdays, I would work security at the recreation center where my daughter had swim practice and start my shift at 1800 (6:00 p.m.) and get off shift at midnight or 0100 hours (1:00 a.m.), depending on the night.

The next day started at 0600 hours (6:00 a.m.), and I would do it all over again. The feelings of abandonment came on, and there was little or no communication with my wife other than me complaining about the cost of mail-order packages left on the front porch every day or insisting that my wife come out and eat dinner at the table with the family rather than staying in her room, eating in her bed.

It was easy to blame this situation on my wife's depression, and there is no question that played a huge role, but looking back, I felt abandoned and lonely. I quit talking, and then I quit trying. Working, kids, cleaning, working, cooking, kids, working. That was my life every day, and I was so tired, but I was surviving and taking care of the kids. This went on for eight long years. When my youngest was nine years old, I had had enough.

I started venting to my oldest daughter, who is in high school now. She was frustrated with her mother also. She and her sister had taken over much of the mother role in the family. I had no one else to talk to, but looking back, I would not do that again. It fed her dissatisfaction with her mother and it was demeaning to her mother, her, and me. Running from job to job did not allow me the time to build friendships or relationships. I didn't have anyone else to talk with, and instead of finding a friend I spoke to my daughter. That is a choice I regret as it was inappropriate to treat her like a friend and speak out about her mother.

During all of this, my wife's depression went undiagnosed. Her doctors gave her pills for all kinds of illnesses, and she was always sick, but the underlying reason was never mentioned. All I knew was that I was fighting this battle alone. In response, I chose to stop talking about anything. I chose to withdraw and only concentrate on work and taking care of the kids. I allowed my feelings of abandonment, rejection, and exhaustion to overtake me, and I quit on the relationship. I quit talking to my wife, I quit trying, I quit being a husband. We didn't even sleep in the same room.

These feelings showed at work, and I am sure they affected the way I did my job. I just wanted one place to escape and would do anything to keep things calm. I felt like a failure and became hypersensitive to criticism as my life was falling apart in the personal realm. My sergeant was still hard to deal with, and I just took it. I didn't want to cause any problems. I tested for sergeant twice during my time in Detectives, finishing in the top five candidates both times. One time the department promoted one person, and the other time they promoted two people, but I was not selected. Even though I didn't feel bad about this, I was left on the list both times. I did well and was still hopeful that my turn would come.

CHAPTER 12

WATER

Before entering law enforcement, I had taught scuba diving for several years and had hundreds of hours underwater. One day a sergeant called and asked me to assist with a search for a firearm, which was reported to be in a large, muddy canal that traversed our city. The handgun had been used in an attempted homicide. I threw my scuba gear together, expecting to go underwater, and drove to the scene. When I arrived, I found the sergeant and a couple of other officers waiting patiently in the shade of a tree next to the canal.

It was a hot summer day filled with bright sunlight. I walked a few yards, peered over the dirt embankment, and saw the canal. It was about twenty-five feet wide and eight feet deep. The banks were covered in thick, deep weeds leading down to the bottom. There was muddy, murky water in the canal. The slow trickle of water at the bottom was

73

only knee deep and about five feet wide. When I got there, I was told I had been called because I was the only one in the department who had any experience with search and recovery in the water. The sergeant took us over to her car and pulled out a piece of metal. It was three feet long, six inches thick, and six inches wide with a three-foot-long rope tied to a loop, welded on each end. The metal weighed more than fifty pounds. It was a large magnet.

The sergeant told us we would be dragging this monstrosity through the water, in the hopes of picking up the missing weapon. She assigned this task to me and another officer, who was one of the members of the department SWAT team. He was a real standup guy, strong and in good shape, solid physically and emotionally. We lugged the dead weight of the magnet to the canal, put on hip waders, slid into the water, and each took a hold of a rope on the end of the magnet. He was nearest the bank, and I was in the middle of the canal as we slowly started dragging the solid hunk of metal through the murky water and weeds. It was hard work while we trudged through ankle-deep mud, lugging the unwieldy, heavy magnet. It caught on everything as we dragged it along the bottom. We were soon sweating profusely with the physical effort.

We had been searching for about thirty minutes when my partner pointed excitedly at the canal bank and gasped out, "Sssnaaake." By time I spotted the snake, my partner had dropped his end of the heavy bar of metal into the muddy bottom of the canal and was on the highest point of the bank opposite where the small, harmless, foot-long garden snake had entered the water. The snake deftly wound its way through the water, down the canal away from us, and slithered out of the water, eager to escape from us large intruders. No matter how much we talked and begged, the officer would not come back into the water. I learned that everyone, even the tough-as-nails guys, has a weakness. His weakness was snakes. I also learned that this was an ineffective way to search the water, and I began using my experiences teaching scuba diving to adapt search and recovery methods from the recreational diving world for use in evidence recovery in the law enforcement world. There had to be better tools that were easier to use.

———————

I shared this experience with my wife, and we both laughed like crazy. At the next diving convention, with her approval, I bought an underwater metal detector. I still use it, twenty-five years later. I had no idea how many forensic dive operations it was going to be used on when I purchased it. I supplied it to the Utah Forensic Divers Association, of which I was a founding member. That detector has now been used in more than fifty dive operations and has assisted in finding a number of weapons used in homicides and armed robberies over the years.

On one occasion the Divers Association was working with Salt Lake City PD, looking for a handgun used in an attempted homicide. During that dive op we located the suspect weapon, plus another that was from a cold-case homicide, and another that was never tied to a crime. It is funny that people throw things in the water, thinking that if they can't see it, no one else will either. All in all, I became one of the leading experts in the state on forensic diving operations. I have trained and worked with dive teams in California, Minnesota, Utah, and Wyoming teaching techniques to gather underwater evidence correctly. Sandy Police Department did see the need for a dive team *but* did not support me in this endeavor. I trained other departments' dive teams and worked with them but was forced to use my personal vehicle to go to the crime scenes. I was also forced to use vacation time to go on the dive operations, even though I received many letters of commendation from other departments for my part in the success of those operations.

This experience taught me that everyone has strengths and weaknesses. The officer who had accompanied me that day in the canal was the real deal. He knew and practiced all the proper techniques, whether on patrol or SWAT, and I would feel safe with him backing me up any day. But snakes were it, no way, no how. The dive teams I trained and worked with were the same way. Each person had strengths, and each had weaknesses. We planned the dives and dive schedules according to those strengths and weaknesses. Some of the guys were great, no matter what the conditions. Some weren't as comfortable in the zero-visibility situations we often encountered. In those situations, we would have them be surface support which they were comfortable and competent at. Then, when the scene was cleared, we would put them in the water to do some training. We did this so they could overcome their weakness and turn it into a strength.

The police department was faced with a similar challenge. Each person, department, and division within the department had strengths and weaknesses. The true leaders developed their people and enhanced those people's skills, while the poor leaders simply passed them off to someone else, pushed them out of the department, berated them, or ignored them.

CHAPTER 13

BUCKETS

The owner of a large complex of storage units made a spot inspection of his property and found several things wrong. He complained to code enforcement and the police department. He was alarmed that many of the tenants were creating fire hazards in their units and did not want his business to burn down. An officer was dispatched to check out the situation, and after seeing a couple of serious problems he thought outside the box. He called the fire department, who responded to do an official fire inspection. The officer stayed to assist. As the fire department went from unit to unit, they would take care of any hazard they saw, as long as it wouldn't damage the unit renter's property or belongings. They opened and closed dozens of units, fixed minor hazards, or left notices for the renter on the storage unit door to fix problems.

When the door of a unit near the rear of the complex was opened, the fire marshal looked in, and his jaw gaped open in amazement. He couldn't believe that the electrical breakers had not tripped from what he saw. The renter of this unit had no electrical outlets. Instead, he'd bought an outlet that screwed into the overhead light, like a lightbulb. There were four places to insert plugs, one on each side. It also had a place to screw in a lightbulb. There were four heavy, orange extension cords plugged in. Each cord led to a freezer. There was an upright freezer on the left, two chest freezers against the back wall, and a cord leading to the right and lying on the ground, as if something (possibly another freezer) had been removed.

Not wanting to damage any property by unplugging the hazardous electrical setup, they opened the freezer on the left to see if the power could be unplugged without ruining anything. It contained three five-gallon paint buckets. They then opened the two chest freezers and were overwhelmed with the stench and odor. The sweet, pungent smell of marijuana spread quickly through the storage unit. They shut the freezers, and the officer quickly called detectives.

I was assigned to park my unmarked car at the entrance to that storage unit and stand there, in the heat of the summer day, with my department-issued Remington 870 shotgun to protect the scene while a search warrant was obtained. There were no laptop computers at that time, so obtaining a warrant was going to take some time. The warrant had to be typed, then driven to a judge in Salt Lake City, seventeen miles away. Then it had to be driven back before we could search. Apparently both chest freezers were full of marijuana. With that amount, we knew the owner was some sort of dealer. With that knowledge, standing there alone, my mind wandered. I kept thinking, *How am I going to stop the dealer with just a shotgun? They will probably have fully automatic weapons. If someone comes back to the storage unit, I am in big trouble.* I envisioned several scenarios, none ending in my favor, but tried to imagine how I could inflict maximum damage and protect myself as best as possible. Time stood still, and even though I was only alone for about two hours it felt like forever.

No bad guys came, and the warrant was obtained. We searched the unit and found more than 600 pounds of marijuana in the freezers. It was packed in several layers of cellophane and about the size of an old hay bale. Each bale was about two-feet long and a foot-and-a-half wide and high. The paint buckets were full of cash wrapped in sandwich baggies and labeled. There was $10,000 to $20,000 in each baggie, totaling $860,000 in cash.

We didn't have any department vehicles large enough to transport that much marijuana, so we used a Chevy Blazer owned by one of our records clerks. The Blazer was full, from front to back, filling all the seats from floor to ceiling. It was so full that we had to use our shoulders to force the doors shut. The only place not filled was the driver's seat. It was the largest drug bust in the state at the time, and all of us received a commendation for our involvement. The money was seized and placed in a trust that has funded the citywide DARE program to educate kids in the city schools about the dangers of drugs. To my knowledge, the money is still funding that program, twenty years later.

The information gathered from this storage unit led to several other search warrants and the arrest of the dealer. He had some duplexes, multiple homes, cars, and a large cabin cruiser boat, all purchased with the drug money. I was particularly interested in the large cabin cruiser, which he took to Lake Powell during the summer. We located it in storage in the city and obtained a warrant to search it. It was getting dark as we stepped up on the deck at the stern and walked forward to the cabin. As we descended the three steps into the cabin, we saw the kitchen area with a dining table to the right. The table was covered with white powder. We tested the powder and yes, it was cocaine. We found out that the dealer used this boat to party with his friends and conceal his people as they packaged cocaine into sellable-sized packages.

––––––––––

This bust was a big deal at the time. I remember many arguments about the drug money, since everyone wanted some of it. The sheriff's department, the district attorney, the DEA, everyone. Gotta love politics. As mentioned above, Sandy City got the majority and used it in a positive way in the community. I was really excited to be part of this bust. This was earlier in my time in Detectives before I shut down and communication had ceased. I shared this experience with my wife. It's always easier to share good news that is exciting. I had not built too many walls at this point, and we still were open and shared things.

CHAPTER 14

AN EVIL PERSON?

There was one case that really hit close to home and hurt me and my family. It hurt me because I was a trained detective and never saw it coming. It hurt my family because of the close proximity and the close relationship we had with the victim. She was like a second mother to my daughters.

My wife and I both worked, and we relied on a woman in the neighborhood to babysit our daughters. Our daughters were six and four at the time and spent the next several years at this daycare, which was a couple of city blocks from our home. The owner and her family had come to the United States from Columbia in South America and worked hard to successfully assimilate into American society. I was told that the owner's husband had been a successful engineer in Colombia. They had three children, two girls in high school and a boy who was about five years younger. They lived in what we called a "county island" within our city, about two blocks from my home. A county island is an area of homes, usually two or three blocks in diameter, that is not incorporated into the city but is considered part of the county and receives its public services from the county, even though it is completely surrounded by the city.

The mother started a daycare within their home, and her daughters assisted her when they were home. The family was active in the local church and well liked. This woman was very caring and did an excellent job, and the daycare was very successful and always full. She and the daycare were a fixture in the neighborhood and loved by all.

One night many years after our daughters had graduated from daycare, Salt Lake County sheriffs were called to the home. The son, who was in his early twenties by this point, had called 911 to report that he had found his father dead from a gunshot wound. The father was discovered sitting in a chair in the living room with a gunshot wound to his head. The weapon was located scattered around the living room in pieces. This obviously brought up questions about how a dead person could disassemble a weapon. The son told the investigators that he was so upset when he found his father that, without thinking, he had taken the gun apart and thrown the parts around the room before calling 911. This was plausible but seemed unlikely. These statements and a few other behaviors didn't add up to the investigator, but the death was ruled to be a suicide. The father was a good and proud man, and this ruling never made sense to me. His wife was like a second mother to my kids, and my wife and I did what we could to help her out. My wife gave her emotional support, and we sent over prepared meals for the family.

A few months later, as this family was in the process of putting their life back together, a fire broke out at their home in the early morning hours of a warm summer night. When the first officer arrived at the scene, he could see smoke and flames. According to the officer, the son was standing in the front yard watching. The officer ran into the house and roused the rest of the family, allowing them to escape frightened but unharmed. Eventually the fire spread from the carport area, throughout the structure, and damaged the entire house.

The son said he had tried to go inside but couldn't, and that he had yelled to wake his family, but they didn't hear him. Investigators determined that the fire was arson and had been started with the use of an accelerant on the side of the house near the carport.

The home was insured, but it was going to take time to repair the damage and rebuild the home. It was not habitable. The mother was concerned about "her" kids in her daycare and on a lesser note, making enough money to survive. She moved into a home about two blocks away in the same area so she would not inconvenience her clients and could continue to run her daycare while her home was being restored.

One day officers were called to this new location to investigate. I was requested to go to the scene. At this time, I was working property crimes, along with some work with the narcotics unit and vice, so I was surprised to be called to the scene of a suspicious death. I heard later that the suspect told officers he knew me, which was why I was called, but have not been able to verify that information. This crime hurt. It tore apart a family that was loved by everyone in the area and tore apart a neighborhood.

I didn't recognize the house. My kids were in high school at this point and hadn't stayed at the daycare for years. I realized I was standing in the home that the daycare had moved to, and there was the mother, dead on her bedroom floor. She had been strangled. Her body was discovered by a relative who had showed up to work in the daycare with her. This was obviously a crime of passion, up close and personal. The son showed up at the house, shortly after police arrived. He had new scratches on his face, suggesting a struggle. The scratches were at an angle that suggested he'd been scratched by someone defending themselves and fighting for their life.

I had to immediately remove myself from this case since I knew the family. The detectives who worked the case did an excellent job. I did drive the young man to the office to be interviewed. That was one of the longest drives I have ever made. For years, his mother had been like a second mother to my daughters. I was sure the son had committed this horrible crime, forcefully strangling his mother. I acted friendly, as an old friend of the family would. Although I wanted to ask so many questions, I couldn't without jeopardizing the case. Instead, we talked and chatted about mundane things unrelated to the case. He acted as if it were a normal day and there was nothing wrong.

In one of his statements to detectives, this young man said he had received the scratches on his face during a pickup basketball game at the community college that he now attended. The angle of the scratches did not match, so that story was discounted. The angle was more consistent with being inflicted by somebody who was reaching over their head and shoulders, clawing and trying to fend someone off and get away. Everybody at the scene felt that he was our likely suspect in this case.

The young man was tried, found guilty, and sentenced to thirty years in prison. During this case, one sister insisted he was innocent and paid for one of the best defense attorneys in the state. He claimed diminished mental capacity and negotiated the charges down from murder to manslaughter. The other sister felt he had killed their mother. This created a rift and tore the family apart. I only hoped the relationship could be rebuilt and repaired later.

During this investigation, the county sheriffs looked at the reported suicide of the father again. I learned they now had doubts it was a suicide and suspected the son had killed his father. Since he was already sentenced to thirty years, the county did not reopen the case. What was his motive to kill his mother? I'm still not sure, but it was reported that he wanted to move back in and live with his mother. When she refused, he grabbed a nearby belt in the heat of the moment and strangled her. He was suspected of homicide in the death of his father, suspected of burning the house down and leaving family inside, then convicted in the death of his mother but pled down to lesser charges because of mental defect. Was this evil or mental illness? We will never know, since he was released from prison and died a few years later.

———————

My wife and I talked emotionally about this case a lot, since it was close to home. I could tell I was getting pretty walled off at this time as she cried, almost uncontrollably, and I did not show a single emotion. Inside I hurt and wanted to hurt whoever did this, but I never showed a thing on the outside. I felt I had to be strong for my kids and my wife. This terrible crime affected my kids, who had all stayed at the daycare for years. The owner was very close to them, and we were friends with the family as well. All of these crimes swirling around one person seemed to indicate a cruelty and self-centeredness that was hidden for years. In fact, they were hidden so well that no one looked at him as a suspect in the early crimes. I am sure there were signs that may have been hidden within the family. That may have been the reason Mom would not let the son move back in. This is only speculation on my part, but I felt guilty that I had not seen it earlier as a seasoned investigator. Unfortunately, hindsight is 20/20, and after the fact it was very clear. I am really sad for the sisters and how this terrible crime destroyed their relationship, but I am really happy that he was put away for a long time. While writing this book, I found out that he had been released from prison early and died in 2018. Whether his crimes were evil, or the result of mental illness is irrelevant, since his actions were truly despicable.

An interesting side note: I had blocked this experience out and only briefly thought about it over the years, always pushing it away. I had hardened myself so much that I would not allow myself to feel anything about it. As I spent time writing, this case suddenly came to me, and I wrote it down. While doing so, my eyes welled with tears. *They* began trickling down my cheeks. My heart rate increased dramatically until I could feel it thud in my chest, unlike the regular rhythm that I take for granted. My emotions went sideways, taking me on a rollercoaster of old feelings I hadn't thought about or expressed in years. Yes, these events affected me in those past years and occasionally return to affect me today. I am fortunate that when something triggers a memory, I am usually awake and can manage it. Occasionally the memory returns as a dream/nightmare that drives me upward, out of bed like a rocket, shaking and drenched in sweat.

There are several things we can do to minimize the effects of such traumatic incidents. One option is journaling. Write the experiences down to get them out. This is a common tool used by counselors and helps get the feelings out. The writing process will bring up feelings but will also make them easier to talk about later. A second option is to talk about the experience with someone you trust. This could be a counselor, a peer-support team member, a friend, or a coworker. Choose someone who will listen and let you work through the feelings you have. If we don't get these feelings out, we are more likely to develop PTSD. If we don't share, we are putting up barriers to communication, which leads to problems in our relationships.

CHAPTER 15

CHEVY'S RESTAURANT

A quiet night in Sandy City, a sleepy suburb of Salt Lake City, was about to change into one of the most confusing and brutal nights in the history of the city. Quinn Martinez** was at the Extended Stay Motel with his girlfriend, Jamie Lucero, and his sister SeAnn Martinez and another friend. They were partying, drinking, and doing drugs. This alcohol/meth-fueled haze had been going on nonstop for several days, the last of which had been at this motel. Jamie had borrowed a car from a friend, and now that friend wanted his car back. Jamie did not respond to his phone calls, so the friend called Quinn in a fit of anger. Quinn took the call and the full brunt of the friend's anger. Now, in his own fit of anger, he stalked back into the room and started a heated argument with Jamie.

PART ONE

The argument was not going well. Quinn told her, "You better shut up, or I'm going to blast you."

Jamie responded in an icy manner. "Do what you gotta do." Quinn did. Blood splattered around the bed and the room as the bullet struck Jamie's upper right leg. This was bad, but this was only the beginning. Then he pointed the gun at her body and said, "I should kill you."

Quinn peeked out the motel room door and formulated a plan. He was relieved when he looked down the hall and saw that no other guests were really paying attention as they moved up and down the hallway, on the way to their rooms. The sound of the gunshot, so loud as it had reverberated in the enclosed room, had caused little disturbance in the hallway. In fact, only a couple of people had turned their head toward the room. Instead of shooting Jamie again, Quinn rapidly left the motel room.

Wounded, Jamie hobbled along. With the assistance of SeAnn Martinez, she slowly made her way to an exterior stairwell, into the parking lot, and toward SeAnn's car. SeAnn wanted to get Jamie to a hospital. Quinn suddenly appeared from another set of stairs, on a mission to intercept them, and fired a shot from the gun that was still in his hand. The aggression Quinn showed was shocking to them, and the women quickly jumped into the car and locked the doors as Quinn yelled, "I'm going to kill you if you don't give me the keys."

SeAnn sped from the parking lot at high speed, leaving her brother behind. She was taking Jamie to the hospital, but not the closest one in Sandy City. They drove all the way across the valley north and west, to West Valley City, and went to a hospital there. They knew questions would be asked, and SeAnn did not want the police to respond and catch her brother. They were very nondescript about the motel and even its location as they dealt with ER personnel.

Meanwhile, Quinn started looking for an escape vehicle, and the rampage began. There were several restaurants nearby, and he walked to the parking lot of the closest, Chevy's Fresh Mex Restaurant, at 7475 South Union Park in Sandy.

PART TWO

Quinn entered the restaurant and asked to use the phone at the desk in the front lobby. An employee, Josh Parker, told him, "That phone doesn't dial out."

In a louder voice, demanded, "Where's a phone that does work?"

"There's a pay phone behind you. You can use that one."

Quinn insisted, "You're lying! Let me use it!"

The ruckus drew the attention of the restaurant manager, Jason Rasmussen, and as a good manager he responded. The drugs in Quinn's system continued their work, and he became increasingly frustrated with the situation as Rasumssen confirmed that he would have to use the pay phone.

Paranoia, common with meth use, kicked in and Quinn said, "You're lying." He reached inside his shirt and pulled out his handgun.

He pointed the weapon at the manager's head and said, "Give me the phone or I'm going to shoot you." As Quinn continued pointing the weapon, Rasmussen ducked behind the hostess desk. He said to Quinn, "Don't shoot me, I'll find you a phone." Quinn lowered the weapon at the crouching manager and pulled the trigger. The manager slid to the floor. The waiter, Josh Parker, witnessed the entire incident from a few feet away and turned in fear to run to the rear of the restaurant. Quinn shot him too and walked out of the front entrance into the parking lot, now looking for a car to steal.

PART THREE

As Quinn stalked out of the restaurant, he saw a man (Richard Reep) backing his car slowly out of a parking space. Inside the car was

Reep's daughter and an elderly relative. The three had just finished dinner with family for a birthday celebration. Reep heard popping noises as he backed up but had no idea what they were. As he began to pull forward, heading to the parking lot exit, a man suddenly appeared in front of his car and yelled, "Give me the car, get out of the car," in a crazed manner. The man had a gun hugged against his chest. Then he put one hand out, like a cop stopping traffic, and pointed the weapon at Reep. In a moment of clarity, Reep knew he had to get out of there. He momentarily slowed with the man in front of him, but as Quinn stepped from the front of the car to the driver's side door, Reep slammed his foot down on the gas pedal and sped away.

PART FOUR

Still without a ride to escape the turmoil he had created, Quinn's journey now crossed paths with Peter Berg and his twelve-year-old daughter, Whitney. Peter and Whitney had just gotten into the car as they left a birthday party for Peter's son/Whitney's older brother. As Peter casually put on his seat belt and prepared to start the car, the passenger door was forcefully yanked open. There stood Quinn with a gun, hovering menacingly over Whitney. Quinn gave a brusque order: "Get out of the car," and then without waiting for a response yelled, "Get out of the car!"

In the driver's seat, Peter worried for his daughter's safety. He slowly got out of the car. Frightened, Whitney followed the example of her father and quickly hurried out of her side of the car.

Quinn yelled to Peter, "Give me the keys!" as he strode around the back of the car with the gun in his hand.

In an act of defiance, Peter threw the keys away from the car and Whitney. Immediately, Quinn raised the weapon and rapidly fired two shots into Peter's chest then watched as Peter collapsed onto the asphalt.

Quinn scurried around like a frightened animal, looking for the keys on the ground but couldn't find them in the dark. He returned to Peter, lying wounded on the ground, and demanded, "Go get the keys." Peter struggled and started to rise, then pointed away from his car and daughter, saying, "They're over there."

Again, Quinn yelled at Peter. "Go get the keys!" Peter slumped back to the asphalt, losing consciousness.

Whitney ran back toward the restaurant in a panic, screaming for help. Instead of continuing to look for the missing keys, Quinn switched his attention to another possible target.

PART FIVE

During this time Debbie Briggs and her adult daughter had pulled into the parking lot on their way to dinner. As they pulled into a parking spot and turned off the car, Debbie saw a lot of movement and action and what looked like an argument at the entrance to the restaurant. Then she saw flashes and realized a gun was being fired. She yelled to her daughter, "Let's get out of here!" She quickly restarted the car, but as she was putting it into reverse, a shadowy apparition appeared at her driver's side window. Quinn had found his next victim and raced over to take the car. He yelled, "Get out of the car," as she hurriedly slammed the car into gear. Briggs stomped on the gas and quickly started to drive away when Quinn shot his weapon through the driver's side window striking Briggs in the face. In pain and rapidly losing blood, she drove a block and half to a Maverick convenience store, where she slid from the car and begged for help. Police were notified, and within minutes an army of officers had arrived. However, in that short time Quinn had vanished from the restaurant parking lot, like a wisp of smoke in the wind.

Now there was even more confusion. The restaurant was in an unusual location in Sandy City, at the corner of the city in a triangle-shaped lot. On the back side of the restaurant was a small hill that dropped off into a neighborhood in Salt Lake County. Across the parking lot at the north edge of the property was the city border separating Sandy City and Midvale. The wounded Josh Parker had continued running out the back of the restaurant, where he tumbled down the hill and collapsed in the back yard of a home in Salt Lake County. The Maverick Store that Debbie Briggs pulled into and collapsed at was in Midvale. Now we had three different jurisdictions and three different law enforcement agencies with gunshot victims and no cumulative knowledge of what had really occurred.

I lived a few blocks from the scene and was one of the first detectives to arrive. Homicide detectives soon arrived and took over the case, but I was assigned several tasks to assist them. When I pulled up to the scene, I saw Midvale Police vehicles, officers, and detectives across the street, parked at the curb, and lined up bumper to bumper. They had responded to the shooting and were offering their assistance as they realized they were dealing with a Sandy PD case. They assisted Briggs, got her to the hospital, and questioned her and her daughter to gain suspect information. Then they worked to make sure Sandy PD detectives had the information they needed.

Salt Lake County Sheriffs were notified by the homeowner whose lot backed up to Chevy's. When deputies arrived, they found a gunshot victim (Parker) with a life-threatening wound. When police saw the flood of flashing lights at the top of the hill above them, they immediately drove to that scene next. The sheriff showed up and immediately demanded to take over the investigation. He went nose to nose with the Sandy chief of police who, after a loud argument, prevailed. Salt Lake County reluctantly agreed to assist, and their deputies and detectives made sure Sandy Detectives had all of the information they needed to fully investigate the case.

I was assigned to go to the home of Quinn's parents in the southwest corner of Salt Lake Valley to see if he had showed up there. At this time, we only knew there had been a shooting with multiple victims; many of the details above were unknown. We knew that SeAnn had picked up Jamie Lucero at the motel and had taken her to the hospital, but that was the extent of our information.

When I arrived at the residence, I was allowed in and found SeAnn and her parents sitting in the living room. It was obvious they didn't really want me there. After some small talk and a lot of convincing, they let me into the closed garage, where SeAnn's car was parked. I could see blood on the passenger side floorboard and passenger seat through the closed car window. The car doors were locked, so I asked for permission to search the vehicle. That request was firmly refused, and the family asked me to leave. When I got to my car, I called my sergeant and asked about getting a warrant since I knew these people were not being honest and were hiding something. I was told not to worry about it by the sergeant and was told to go to the University Hospital in the northeast part of the Salt Lake Valley, where Jason Rasmussen, who had died, had been transported. I drove the twenty miles with a heavy heart because I knew I was going to the hospital for one thing and one thing only: to gather the bullet from Jason's body so it could be booked into evidence to convict the suspect in this horrific crime. After waiting several hours, that task was complete, and I returned to the office to book evidence and do reports on my activities of that night. It was a long day. By the time I got home, I was exhausted and really wanted to get some sleep. I had been up for over twenty-four hours, had driven from one end of the valley to the other and back again, had dealt with several uncooperative people, and then had done my reports. My wife knew I had been involved with something major since I was not the on-call detective that week but still was called out (as was every detective in the department who was available). We talked about the crazed guy who had shot his girlfriend then tried several times to carjack different cars so he could escape, ultimately shooting four or five people. At that time, things were still unclear on the totality of the incident. I was shocked at how such a thing could happen in this quiet town and only a few blocks from my home.

As the case developed and more information was shared, it became even more frightening. I had neighbors ask questions about the suspect and what he could have been thinking. It was frustrating to not be able to answer and to realize that they thought I could understand the mindset of this killer. It was also frustrating and scary to see what drugs, especially meth, can do to a somewhat normal person. This was still early in my time as a detective, so I was still fairly open with my wife. I didn't share any details but gave her a general outline of what had happened and of the role I took, where I went, and what I did.

The day after the shootings, Quinn was located in a friend's basement apartment, where a SWAT team had him cornered. The house was about a block from the Maverick store. He came to the bottom of the stairs with a knife in his hand. He advanced up a couple of the steps, but when ordered, with several weapons pointed at him, he dropped the knife and was taken into custody. I was happy Quinn was captured and later convicted. It was nice to know I had contributed to the case, even in a small way.

———————

The trauma to the victims in this case is horrendous and ongoing. The families of the two men murdered by Quinn still grieve but go on with their lives. The two wounded victims are physically healed and carry on. They have told the local newspaper that this experience is something that will never leave them. I am sure there are many levels of PTSD in the people that were victims and many of those who witnessed the incident.

I have discovered that everyone in life experiences some sort of trauma. Most experiences are not as severe as this one, which was similar to the experiences of public safety personnel. These people have shown great resilience and have done so by following different principles and techniques they have learned to work through the pain. In many cases this is a process that can take years. Let's take a brief look at some of those techniques and principles:

It all starts with admitting that there is a problem, which is part of being self-accountable. Then we have to talk about it and get the feelings out. This could mean talking to family, coworkers, counselors, or therapists. Whatever works for the individual is just fine. I know many of the victims and witnesses in this case spent time in counseling and therapy.

We must also take action and learn different techniques. Public Safety uses post-incident debriefings for this purpose. This is a good start, but in my opinion these debriefings are too brief and limited to really address the underlying issues. I know that when I finally went to counseling, it took several months but was well worth the time.

**Names are used in this chapter as they were printed in the Salt Lake Tribune where much of this information was verified.

CHAPTER 16

VICE

W hile in Detectives, I had the opportunity to do some work with the Vice unit on some "hooker stings." The first time, I was put up in an inexpensive motel room in a rougher part of town, and calls were made to set up appointments with the girls. The room was equipped with a microphone. Each room had one door leading to the outside, so the takedown team was stationed in the next room and would move outside my door after the suspect entered my room. Since it was the middle of July, we decided to use the phrase *Merry Christmas* as the takedown signal. This meant that if I used the phrase *Merry Christmas*, the arrest or takedown team was supposed to come into my room and take the suspect into custody.

The first woman arrived, and I shut the door and moved to the center of the room near the bed.

She said, "What can I do for you?"

I paused and said to her, "What will you do?"

She looked at me in a questioning way and asked, "You're not a cop, are you?"

I laughed and responded, "Are you crazy?"

She then told me, "You know, if you are you have to tell me. And if you are a cop, you can't lie."

I just laughed and firmly replied with a couple of expletives to emphasize, "no, I'm not a pig."

She answered, "Okay, I just don't want to get busted."

I laughed again and told her, "You've been watching too much of that show *Cops*." No, I'm not a cop, and I don't want to get busted either."

We talked a little more and made an agreement to have either sex for $100 or a blow job for $50.

I responded, "Merry Christmas, and you're hot too."

Nothing happened, and she started taking off her blouse

Now starting to get nervous at the lack of response, I said, "Dang, it's my lucky day. Merry Christmas to me."

And still nothing happened.

Now my mind started working overtime. I was thinking, *What the heck, how many times can I say Merry Christmas in the middle of July before she gets more suspicious, and where the crud are the guys?* All sorts of scenarios were running through my mind. I wondered if the mic had quit working.

Finally, when she had stripped down to her underwear, I realized the team was not coming in. I reached down where I had hidden a pair of handcuffs and my badge and let her know, "Yes, I am a detective, and you are under arrest."

I handcuffed her, sat her on the bed, and opened the door. There was the takedown team, rolling on the ground outside the room, laughing as they told me, "Hey dude, you sounded a little surprised and nervous in there."

The only thing I could say was, "You jerks" with a sheepish grin on my face. I found out this was typical for a first time bust, and now I was initiated.

On another occasion we set up in a higher-end hotel I was posing as an out-of-town businessman and started calling escort services. On this day we would bust the suspect, then walk her through the adjoining room door where other detectives had the recording equipment and the court paperwork.

One escort who used the name Summer came into the room. She was in her early twenties with blond hair and blue eyes. She was very attractive but acted a little hesitant and shy. Her mannerisms and behavior told me that she was really new at this. We talked about having sex, and she was hesitant, so I asked her about getting a blow job or a hand job instead. She really didn't answer but said, "Why don't we start with a back rub first and see where it goes? I have some really nice Avon lotion." I agreed, took off my shirt, and lay face down on the bed. She took off her outer clothing down to her underwear and began putting lotion on my back and giving me a back rub. I really made it sound good as I talked softly to her, moaning a little and saying, "Dang, that really feels good." This went on for about fifteen minutes until my sergeant, who was listening in the next room, got nervous. He could hear our conversation, but the video had malfunctioned. She was finally ready to agree to a transaction when the side door to the room unexpectedly opened, and the sergeant led the arrest team in. He had gotten nervous about liability and whether something might happen that would affect my marriage. He felt he couldn't wait any longer. Summer sat on the side of the bed as she put her clothing back on. I asked her why she was doing escort work, and she told me, "For the money." Her managers had offered her a lot of money. I then asked her how long she was going to do this without performing sexual acts and she told me she didn't know. She hadn't thought about it. I let her know that it was only a matter of time before having sex would be forced on her by her bosses or a customer, in order to earn that good money and it would be sooner than later. I let her know she needed to think hard and decide if this was a road she wanted to continue on. We cited her for doing business without a license and sent her on her way. I did gain a whole new appreciation for Avon lotion, however.

I looked out the window of the motel room, at the parking lot drenched in sunlight. I saw the next escort parking her car and walking into the hotel. I found it kind of funny that they all parked within a few parking places of each other and that they all dressed the same. After the third escort arrest, in rapid succession, I asked one of the other detectives to take my place and give me a break. I then took his place on the arrest and backup team.

As we listened and watched the conversation, the escort entered the room. She asked him what he would like her to do. He kind of stuttered and stammered a little. She then told him the cost would depend on what he wanted her to do. He hemmed and hawed some more. It was obvious that all he had to do was tell her he wanted sex and then she would give him a price, but he wouldn't ask. After what seemed like an eternity of this back and forth, I finally took a pizza delivery box that was left over from lunch and still contained half a pizza, then "delivered" it to his door. I knocked, announcing, "Domino's Delivers." He opened the door and looked at me with a puzzled look on his face. I handed him the pizza and quickly whispered, "Dude, just ask her for sex and how much it will cost." I pretended to take some money from him, turned, and walked to the room next door. He took the pizza, closed the door, and laid the pizza box on the counter in his room. He asked the woman if she would have sex with him, and she accepted and named her price. She was then arrested. This detective was new and had misunderstood entrapment. He was under the impression that if he asked for sex, it would be entrapment. We later explained that asking for sex and the suspect naming a price was not entrapment. On the other hand, if he had offered her $100,000 for sex and she had accepted, that would be entrapment. We laughed about the sexy pizza delivery for a long time.

I was surprised that the sergeant was actually worried about my wellbeing. Given my prior experiences, I was suspicious, thinking he didn't trust me to do the right thing. I later realized he was really watching out for me and that his brusque manner was just a wall, to protect himself from being hurt.

In my limited experience, women in the sex industry are trapped there because they are either really desperate or have made stupid choices that didn't work out. They throw away their self-esteem, their health, and safety for money. They end up with little money and end up in a life that is mentally and emotionally damaging.

People need a sincere, caring connection with others. Sadly, by this point in my marriage I was living a lie, just like these women. Just as they were trapped by their earlier choices, I was trapped by mine—or at least I felt trapped and didn't see a way out. We all get to this point sometime in life. It may not even be a serious problem, but we can feel trapped in our job, in our career, or in our relationships with others. We can even be trapped, to some degree, in our interactions with colleagues who may also feel trapped in their interactions with us. We can be trapped in a number of different roles in life and not even realize it. Of course, PTSD itself is a trap—one that you might feel can't be escaped. The thing about traps is that we can escape them with the right tools, the right outlook, the right attitude. However, it does take courage and determination, as well as being proactive.

We must be self-accountable to look inside ourselves and have enough courage to see and admit what is happening and what we are feeling. We need to be determined enough to act on what we see. This action requires us to be proactive and seek out people we can talk to and who can assist us. Then we must take the steps we need to heal. When we do this, we are no longer victims. Instead, we transform ourselves into powerful healers. First, we heal ourselves, and then we can start healing our damaged relationships as we chose.

Unfortunately, I was not able to do this with my wife. Instead, I built a bedroom in the basement, which was where I slept now. My relationship with my wife was gone. She stayed in her room. I took care of the kids and worked. We didn't talk about anything.

The walls were complete and were not coming down.

CHAPTER 17

OLYMPICS

During the 2002 Salt Lake City Winter Olympics I was selected to be on the Dignitary Protection Team. This entailed working with the Secret Service and transporting selected world leaders to various venues and locations. For eight days, I provided service to the president of Finland and also provided guidance to the vice president of Czechoslovakia.

My department went to one week of training to learn how to do our jobs. Then we filled in for the Utah Highway Patrol members in each county while they did their training. We covered Wasatch, Summit, Utah, Salt Lake, and Davis Counties for a week each. Our assignment was to cover the county for UHP and in our spare time to scout all possible routes to the different event venues that we might need to know. This wasn't too difficult, although I soon realized no one could pay me enough to be a trooper.

One night in Weber County, one of our officers was checking on a suspicious vehicle in a parking lot up Weber Canyon, on the southeast side of the county. As he approached the car on foot, a gunshot rang out, and the back window of the suspect vehicle shattered. He quickly dove to the ground and scrambled across the dirt parking lot, looking for cover and calling on his radio for backup as he did so. He found some rocks lined up and large enough to protect himself and hunkered down with his weapon drawn, looking for the threat and waiting for the cavalry to arrive. He couldn't tell if the shot had come from the car or if some unknown person on the nearby mountain had shot at him or the car. He wasn't sure where the threat was coming from.

When we found out that one of our brothers was under fire, we all took off as fast as we could to get there and back him up. I was in the northwest part of the county, but I had good clear roads to get there quickly. I soon found out something about my patrol vehicle that I was not aware of. I accelerated quickly, then my engine sputtered and quit. My speed dropped to eighty-five miles per hour, and I stomped on the gas again and took off. Then the engine sputtered, and once again my speed dropped. For some unfathomable reason there was a governor on my engine, which automatically shut my car down at ninety-seven miles per hour. After my car shut down for the third time and I began hearing other officers announcing their arrival at the scene on the radio, I realized that I was going to be covering the county roads while the others worked at the scene. Talk about frustrating.

It turned out that the man in the driver's seat of the suspicious car had used a high-powered rifle to commit suicide. The bullet had come out through the back window of the car, shattering it and going over the approaching officer's head.

During the Olympics, when I wasn't escorting dignitaries, I was assigned to patrol Parley's Canyon. Interstate 80 runs through Parley's Canyon and is the main east/west freeway connecting Salt Lake City and Park City/Heber City areas. When patrolling we were issued an MRE (meal ready to eat) for dinner. I soon learned that some MRE's were okay, and most weren't. I also learned to get to roll call early enough to pick out a decent MRE. After that I was always one of the first there. I got lucky and found an inexpensive apartment near the University. It had been rented by the FBI for agents but was not being used. I spoke to the building manager and rented the apartment for myself. Having an apartment nearby really paid off. I was near enough to my patrol area that I cut out half an hour of travel each way, in good weather. When it snowed, I saved an hour of travel time each way. It was nice to stumble home and enjoy that extra hour of sleep before starting over again. I had no idea how exhausting working twelve hours on, and twelve hours off could be.

When escorting dignitaries, I spent a lot of time in the cold, ice-covered parking lots of different Olympic venues with a Secret Service agent, watching the vehicles. Our caravan usually consisted of me in the lead in my marked patrol vehicle accompanied by a secret service agent in my car. Then an armored Secret Service suburban carrying the VIP's party, and a black Secret Service suburban with at least two agents bringing up the rear. Interestingly, when we got back to the dignitaries' quarters, we were always stopped at a secure entrance gate. The agent in my car would get out and walk to the secure gate. Even though I had been background checked and vetted, I would be shuttled out of a side gate off the premises as the dignitary, agents, and their vehicles were allowed through the secure gate.

I was patrolling Parley's Canyon one day when the Czechoslovakian Nordic Ski Team coach's car broke down on his way to the final event. It was a forty-minute drive from where I picked him up over to Soldier

Hollow, and the gold medal event was scheduled to start in thirty minutes. I was told, "Do what you have to and get him there." I put him in my car and took off, lights flashing and siren blaring. I drove up Parley's Canyon, took the Highway 40 exit to Heber City/Midway, and took the River Road exit, which was faster, and got into the quaint little town of Midway. The spectator traffic on Main Street in Midway going to the venue was bumper to bumper. Rather than create confusion and make it worse, I shut off my lights and siren. I entered the small town, found a side road to go around the traffic. Once I was past the barely moving congestion, I resumed lights and siren and hurried the rest of the way ahead of the snarl of vehicles. I arrived with two minutes to spare. When we arrived, Olympic officials met us and hurried my passenger into the venue. He paused long enough to give me his card and say in accented English, "Thank you, you come to my country, and I show you how we drive."

As I was leaving Midway, near the junction of River Road and Highway 40, I was surprised by a highway patrol sergeant who used the overhead lights on his patrol vehicle to pull me over in my marked patrol vehicle. He came to my window and angrily demanded to know what I was doing. I told him that I had been ordered to get the coach to the venue. The sergeant got even angrier. He demanded to know why no one had contacted him and asked, "Why did you shut your lights and siren off when you got into Midway?" I explained that the traffic was so heavy on the small street that it wouldn't have gotten me through the town any faster and would have been more hazardous by creating confusion with the civilian drivers. He started yelling at me again, asking why he hadn't been notified since he was in charge of this county. I referred him to the sergeant in SLC who had given me my orders. He went back to his car and called. After getting off the phone, he strode back up to my car, anger in each step. He looked at me through my driver's side window and said, "Okay, I'm not happy about it, but you can go." I didn't say a word as I drove away and could only think, *What an egotistical jerk.*

This kind of behavior is common in life, no matter what we are doing. There will be good people and ego-driven jerks. Sometimes they swap roles, and the good person becomes the ego-driven one and vice versa. Sometimes I am in the role of a good person or an egotistical jerk. When this type of behavior is directed at us, it is a good reminder of times we want to temper our own behavior. The feelings I had that day really remind me that I don't want to be "that guy." I want to be a good leader and choose my behavior rather than reacting to a situation in an angry outburst. At that time, I replayed the encounter over and over in my head with the usual, *I should have said this, or I should have done that.* I now know this is unproductive, since the encounter is over, and nothing can be changed.

Now I turn to some coping techniques to calm me down and get me back into a positive mindset. In this case I turned my car radio to my favorite FM station and listened to some of my favorite songs until the angry feelings were gone. Other ways to deal with this type of situation are positive self-improvement tapes or CDs or downloads. I have a lot on my phone. If there is a safe place and you have the time, you can also do a five-minute meditation. At the end of the day, you could get a long massage to get rid of the tenseness and anxiety. Other ways to work through these feelings are to run or work out. I let this particular incident bother me for a few days. Now I just use it as a learning experience. I learned how I do not want to be. I will not judge that officer, however. He may have been having a bad day. I can look at the results without judgment and see that the way he behaved did not work and is not how I want to be.

———————

I had told my daughter, who was at this time a senior in high school, that I wouldn't move out until she graduated, but I was done with my marriage. The FBI leased a bunch of inexpensive apartments near event venues to house agents. I found one of them that was vacant and not being used. I negotiated with the manager and was able to rent it. It was inexpensive and near the stadium being used for the opening and closing Olympic exercises. I moved out of the house and into the apartment a few days prior to the Olympics. I spoke to my kids and some of the guys I worked with, but that was about it. I worked twelve hours on and twelve hours off.

There were so many things that happened during the Olympics, and it would have been nice to talk about them with someone, but that didn't happen. I worked, slept, got ready to work, and worked. In some respects, this was actually a good way to adjust to a new life after nineteen years of marriage. Even though I wanted the divorce, it was surprising how much it hurt. Even if I had remained in the home we shared, we were past the talking stage since I had built a separate bedroom in the basement. I no longer worked at getting my wife to come out of the bedroom for dinner. I had quit and didn't care because there was no relationship anymore. It was too much work. I cared about the kids and was grateful to my daughters for picking up the slack. The house was never very clean, and I still worked horrible hours, cooked, took care of the kids, and did what I could. My daughters helped as well as teenage girls with busy lives can. My oldest daughter didn't graduate until June, and I broke my word to her, which I deeply regret. When I moved out, I filed for divorce and gave the paperwork to my wife in March of 2002. She started crying and said, "You can't divorce me, I have cancer." While she had used health problems as an excuse for years, this was a new one, and I told her, "No, you don't, you are always using health problems as an excuse and you're just trying to get me to stay." A few days later she brought me paperwork from her doctor. She did have cancer.

I did not turn in the divorce paperwork until a year later so she would have insurance, but I did not move back in. This was an indication of how bad our relationship was. She was going to doctors, finding out she had cancer, and had never said a word to me. If I had known, I would have gone to the doctors with her and would have supported her. I did not know until it was too late. The walls were complete and were not coming down. We spoke about the kids, or spoke in anger, and that was it.

As an interesting side note, we went to marriage counseling a couple of times in the years prior to this. Early in the process, I didn't recognize the mistakes we were making in counseling. We listened to each other, but when we were done, I simply went back to my usual ways. The next time, we were both receptive and listened, but my wife was in such a depressed state that she could not follow through with the suggestions. This taught me a couple of things: Counseling is good, and it works if both parties give one hundred percent and implement the things learned. If we don't take committed action to implement the changes, things will simply stay the same and not improve. It requires personal accountability to implement these new actions. My suggestion is to get counseling if needed. Try it. But know that it will only work if both parties put in the effort; if this is done, counseling will work.

CHAPTER 18

BACK ON THE STREETS

Shortly after the Olympics, after eight years as a detective, I was moved back to patrol. My detective sergeant, after fifteen years in Detectives, was also moved back to patrol. I was assigned to his shift. On my first day back in patrol, he asked to meet me in a church parking lot, and I did. As we sat there in our marked patrol cars, open driver's window to open driver's window, he gruffly told me," I don't expect much from you, but if you cause me any problems, I will make sure you are fired." I listened in disbelief, thinking, *are you kidding me, here we go again. Is this ever going to stop?*

One night, a woman in a neighboring city who had a lengthy prior criminal record used a handgun to shoot at an officer. She was already a wanted person, and that action set the JCAT (Joint Criminal Apprehension Team) directed by the US Marshals Service into action and on her trail. The next morning at about 0800 hours (8:00 a.m.) she was seen in a Maverik convenience store in my city, just off the I-15 freeway at the 9000 South exit. When the task force members, who had been searching for her all night, arrived she was gone, but only by a few minutes. We were asked to assist and set up a perimeter containment. A number of officers started searching the area.

A suspect photo was sent to our laptops from the surveillance camera at the store. In the video, the suspect was wearing a light jacket, pajama bottoms, and what looked like slippers. This was March, in Utah. There was slush on the ground, sleet was falling, and the temperature was between thirty-three and thirty-five degrees. It was cold and slushy. She was definitely underdressed for walking in these conditions. I knew she would not get far.

There was an office/warehouse complex across the parking lot to the south of the convenience store. There were large bays with rollup doors in the back. One of our officers left the convenience store and drove through the business complex. He did not see the suspect. When he stopped by my post on the south side of that business complex to chat, I asked him to watch my spot in containment. I had a feeling she could be found in the complex and drove north through the businesses. The first thing I did was drive past the large rollup bay doors at the back of the buildings. I got out and made sure each was locked and secure. I also checked the man-sized entry doors and made sure they were all locked. When I got to the convenience store parking lot, I turned back south at the front side of the business complex. At the first office I got out, went into the business, and asked for the manager. I asked him if a woman had come into his business and gave him her description. He looked at me with a questioning look in his eyes and told me, "Yes, she is in my office right now using the phone." We peeked around the corner and down the hall. I had him point to his office. The suspect had taken a shot at an officer the night before and was considered armed and dangerous. I had the manager and secretaries leave the office and go outside behind a brick wall. I quietly called out on my radio for backup and then decided that taking her by surprise would be better than dealing with an armed barricaded suspect. I approached the office door and saw the woman standing next to the manager's desk, purse hanging on her arm by a strap. She was talking on the phone with her back to me. Then, she turned. When she saw me, she got a shocked look on her face. I raised my gun and ordered her to get on the ground. She lowered herself to the ground, on her stomach and kept her hands spread wide from her body. Then I took her into custody without incident. I found it funny that I got a letter of appreciation from the US Marshals Service and a coffee cup with their logo simply because I got out of my car and got my feet a little wet. Three or four other officers had driven by looking for the woman, but no one got out to really look. One of my friends who was part of the JCAT team for three years was a little envious. The coffee cup was something they gave out as a reward, but not very often. He had participated in a lot of high-risk cases and revealed that he had never gotten one.

I wasn't divorced or separated when I met a woman who I grew to like. I was kind of in limbo and didn't have a solid adult relationship at this time. I was just working at keeping the relationships with my kids in good shape. My apartment was not nice. It was small, older, and needed some updates, but it was what I could afford. In fact, it was so bad that my daughters wouldn't stay with me and preferred to meet somewhere else. My son, who was in elementary school, loved to come and spend the night with Dad though.

I was really proud of my success at work apprehending the suspect in the business park and the good decisions I had made during this call. I had gone the extra mile with success. Things were starting to flow again. My sergeant couldn't say anything bad about it—I hoped. People at the department were excited as well, and things were looking rosy at work at the time.

CHAPTER 19

THE FOUNTAIN

I t was an early spring morning, still semi dark with frost on the ground
and in the air. As I left roll call that morning, I was dispatched to an
apartment complex regarding a missing three-year-old boy. The parents
had come out of their bedroom and found the front door hanging wide
open. According to the young couple, their child was a tiny Houdini,
a little escape artist, and was constantly getting out. They had even
resorted to putting at least two extra locking devices on the door to stop
him, and he still got out. I arrived and spoke to the parents, getting
information such as a description of the child, the approximate time he
was last seen, what kinds of things he liked to do, the location of nearby
playgrounds, etc.

Another officer arrived, and we started searching the complex. The
first place I looked was the fountain and pond at the main entrance in

front of the manager's office. Some teenagers, who were out having fun, had put soap into the fountain the night before, and this had formed a mountain of soap bubbles. There were so many bubbles, they were overflowing from the fountain onto the parking area. I couldn't even see the water. Two other officers and I continued searching the complex for the next thirty to forty minutes.

When the sun came up, it started to get warm. We paused near the fountain to regroup and redirect our search efforts. A small breeze came up, creating a cool current in the warming air. It also was just enough breeze to part the jiggling soap bubbles. The bubbles parted just enough for a neighbor, who was assisting in the search, to see a child's foot. Then he saw the little body, floating face down in the water. We hurriedly reached in and pulled the boy out of the fountain by the foot. We laid him gently on the ground, and I performed CPR until fire and paramedics arrived. I turned the boy over to the paramedics, and they continued CPR efforts.

The boy was transported to Children's Hospital, with the EMTs working on him all the way there. I met with the family and gave them the information they needed so they could be with their son. I made arrangements for a neighbor to drive them to the hospital, since they were understandably distraught. Unfortunately, the boy did not survive. I held myself together for the family and did my job, but this one hurt badly. When kids are involved, it always does. Luckily, I had a good lieutenant who spoke with me at the scene and recognized the pain I was feeling. He told me to take some time and not worry about my report until I had taken care of myself. I found a nearby church parking lot and went to the farthest back corner, where I could be alone. I sat there in my car and I cried and cried. Once I had the tears out of my system, I bottled the feelings back up, went to the office, did my report, and got back to work.

I was angry at myself and beat myself up for a long time for not seeing the boy in the pond the first time, even though I had looked the best I could. I was angry at the kids who didn't think of the possible consequences when they put the soap in the fountain. I am sure the shiny overflow of bubbles attracted the boy to the fountain, and those bubbles also kept us from seeing the boy in the water and delayed his rescue. I tortured myself wondering if the additional thirty minutes searching were the difference between the life and death of the boy. I was frustrated that CPR didn't bring him back, even though I knew that if the situation calls for CPR, the person is already dead, and it is a miracle to bring them back to life. I hurt for the young couple and the loss they were suffering. It just hurt, through and through.

This experience hurt badly. I had my own kids, even though they didn't live with me. It reminded me of a similar call a few years earlier, when a young boy who was the same age as my son had died in a crib death incident. I hurt for the boy's parents, and I couldn't do anything to make it better. It sucked and I felt so powerless.

Around this time, the woman I had met showed up again. She was vivacious, lively, and exciting. She seemed to like me and wanted to be around me. She did things that I was not used to and was always surprising me. She was everything I thought I was missing with my first wife. One night I was working security at the recreation center, and we ran into each other. After greetings she said, "Hey, you know I've been flirting my tail off with you for months. Are you going to have sex with me or not?" I was stunned and kind of stammered, "I get off work at one." When I left work that night, she was waiting, and thus began the story of wife number two.

At first there was some doubt about our relationship, since she was dating another guy who wanted to marry her. He had money and came from a family that had power. Unfortunately, she ran her own business in Utah, and he lived near Washington, DC. This was a quick transition. We dated, and for some reason she later agreed to marry me. By the time my first marriage came to an end, my first wife and I were not talking, didn't have a physical relationship, and did nothing together anymore. It was the total opposite with this new relationship. This woman was active, worked too much, and was very successful. She had a great laugh and was spontaneous and fun to be around. Yes, this relationship started while I was married. This, in and of itself, should have been a warning sign that I was heading into troubled waters, but I was at such a low point in my life that I chose the new relationship rather than have no relationship. Looking back, I was afraid of being alone. In my first relationship, I had essentially been alone for eight long years, and I didn't want to do that anymore. Upon reflection, I should have spent more time exploring the relationship. At the time, however, my self-esteem was so low that I couldn't believe this beautiful, sexy, successful woman was interested in me. I jumped in, hook, line, and sinker.

I think human beings are hardwired to psychologically crave the feeling of partnership—of finding someone we feel a connection with. The problem is that sometimes our biological needs get in the way. I allowed the trauma I had already experienced and the emotional wounds from my most recent relationship to cloud my judgement. I felt a connection and leapt in. From the beginning we were never really a team. She worked and worked. Making money was her primary focus. I think it fulfilled one of her insecurities. She controlled everything. In the beginning I didn't notice these characteristics and behavior patterns. I just put up with any questionable behavior and followed along. This complacency is one of the symptoms of experiencing traumatic events as described by Dr. Gilmartin in his class and book. I made critical decisions every day at work. When I got home, I didn't want to make any more decisions. I made all of the decisions in my last relationship because I had to, even though I was in survival mode. In this relationship, my new partner happily exerted control, made the decisions, and I allowed it. According to her, she was better at decision making anyway. We both worked hard and took care of our kids, hers and mine. But again, we were never a team.

My oldest daughter was in college at this point. My new wife's son was a senior in high school, and my second daughter was a junior at the same school. The next three children were also close in age in junior high or fifth and sixth grade at the elementary school. My second daughter moved in with us for a few months.

My new wife and I had been married about two years when the cancer took my first wife. My son was eleven at the time, and he moved in with us as well. We didn't have enough rooms for all the kids, so my second daughter, who was now a junior in high school, moved in with her grandparents. When my first wife passed away, it was really hard on my kids. When my son moved in with us, wife number two wholeheartedly took him in and treated him as if he were her own. She counterbalanced me with him. I was hard and demanding, wanting him to be his best. He rebelled, and she had a knack of bonding and getting through to him. I am still grateful for that. She kept a very clean home and was caring and giving to other people, but it had to be anonymous. She gave to her own kids and to Alex, my son.

My son was twelve when he asked me to teach him how to fish. I laughed to stall for time because I hadn't fished since I was a teenager, but I told him, "Okay, I can do that." Then he added, "I want to learn how to fly fish."

Now I was in trouble. I had never fly fished.

I told him, "I have never fly fished, but I know someone who could teach you."

He looked at me and quietly said, "But Dad, I want you to teach me."

I called my friend and I learned to fly fish with my son. I couldn't teach him, but I could learn with him. This turned out to be one of the best things I have done in my life. We went stream fishing for years and never caught much, but we had some great times together.

One day when my son was about fifteen, we decided to go fishing. It was mid-November, but the weather was decent. We found a place on the upper Provo River where the stream flowed in front of us from right to left. It was a flat meadow area, and there was a small rivulet that branched off next to us. It started to snow, but the snow was not sticking to the ground. There were large flakes moving toward the ground, but they disappeared as they hit the ground. My son was on the other side of the rivulet, about twenty feet away from me. It was quiet, the only sound being the ripple of the water in the stream. It was completely peaceful and calm. I cast my line into the river and looked over at him. He was lying on the ground with his feet toward the river, resting on a log. His fishing pole was leaning on another log with the fishing line trailing into the river. He had his hands clasped behind his head and was staring at the slowly drifting snowflakes in the gray sky. I quietly asked, "What are you doing, buddy?"

He slowly turned his head, looked at me, and in a tone just above a whisper said, "Just enjoying this moment, Dad."

This is one memory I will never forget.

———————

My second marriage was a tough relationship. There was a lot of anger on her part and disagreements between us. My wife was good with my son, but there was a lot of resentment toward me, the commitment of marriage, and even the world at large and people in general that slowly began to reveal itself.

I remember an incident when she came home and told me a woman had cut her off in traffic. She followed the woman until the woman flipped her off. Then my wife got angry and pulled up next to her, still driving down the road, and threw her cell phone at the other car. The cell phone broke, and she found pieces of it along the road but could not find her sim card. We narrowed the search area down to a quarter mile area along a busy street and began looking. It took about forty-five minutes, looking through the weeds and dirt in the ditch along the side of the road. I found the sim card. This experience should have been another clue, but I was stubborn and/or stupid and was sure I could make things better. I definitely did not want to go through divorce again. I tried everything I could, but I did not have enough tools in my toolbox to take care of myself, let alone try to fix someone else's problems. I thought I could do this because as a cop, that is what I did: fixed everything around me. The problem was that I was so focused on her problems, I did not even see my own. Later on, when I had recognized and started fixing my own issues, I realized that I couldn't fix someone else. Only they can do that. Some things just aren't fixable, and in hindsight this relationship and some of my wife's problems weren't. At least not by me. I also realized later that we had one thing in common: We both worked too much. It was our way of avoiding dealing with the trauma and feelings we had experienced in our lives. I thought I worked extra hours for all the years of my first marriage to make the money needed to support my family. But another reason was that when I worked, I was focused on work. When I got home after working a sixteen-hour day, I was so exhausted mentally and physically that I would collapse into bed and be gone. There was no time to think, so I didn't. I had a few nightmares when I was younger, but when I retired and suddenly had plenty of time to remember things, I started having more. I have heard this is common with many veterans from the Vietnam war, who are now in their seventies or eighties. They worked so much to keep busy and didn't show any symptoms of PTSD, but when they retire the symptoms start, including nightmares, sweats, and anxiety.

Humans are similar in behavior and keeping busy was one way for me to avoid working through those memories. Deep down I knew there was a problem, but as long as I kept busy, I could avoid it and pretend that the problem wasn't there. At this point in my second marriage, I started working more and looking for things to do. Not for the money but because I did not want to face the past. I also recognized that my present relationship was not pleasant, and I did not want to face that. These are all things that I did not see at the time but have become abundantly clear as I have healed myself.

CHAPTER 20

THE MOUNTAIN ROAD

One day I was dispatched to provide backup to another officer at about 0200 hours (2:00 a.m.). He was in an affluent neighborhood high up on the side of the mountains that bordered the east side of the city. It was a brisk night and just cold enough, even in a long-sleeve uniform with long johns underneath, to feel the chill.

When I got there, his K-9 truck was parked on the right side of the road with his headlights and spotlights on a BMW. The BMW and its two occupants were parked facing him, about a car length and a half in front of him. There was a mountainside to the right of his truck with enough room on the roadway to his left for one car to get by, and a ten- to twenty-foot drop off on the left side of the road. Both vehicles were running. Everyone wanted heat to fight off the chill of the night. The BMW also seemed prepared to make a quick getaway.

The road behind the BMW was a dead end, and the BMW was facing the only way out.

I eased up to the scene, headlights turned off so I wouldn't backlight the officer and possibly make him an easy target. I parked behind the officer and carefully walked up to his driver's window to find out what was going on. He rolled down his window and explained the situation. When he came upon the scene, the girl was parked in the car where it was now, on the wrong side of the road across the street from the houses, facing traffic. As he pulled up, the man in the vehicle had come walking down the driveway from the dark, unlit home. This struck him as suspicious.

As the officer was bringing me up to speed, the BMW suddenly spun its tires in the gravel and sped quickly forward toward the only escape route—the exact spot where I was standing. I don't remember drawing my weapon, but suddenly I was looking over the sights of my handgun at the driver's forehead. I could see the pores in her skin as I stepped back and pulled the trigger. I squeezed and squeezed, and my weapon did not go off. My head was screaming, *go bang, why aren't you going bang, what is wrong with my gun?* My voice was yelling, "Stop, stop the car." I continued stepping back.

As I reached the rear of the K-9 truck, the car skidded to a stop as suddenly as it had started. I bent my knee about two inches forward, shifting my weight, and my knee touched the front bumper. It took me three years to figure out why my weapon did not discharge. I did a lot of reading as a firearms instructor, and one day I came across an article that explained what had happened: When someone has a big enough adrenaline dump in a high stress situation, it's possible to squeeze the grip/handle of the weapon so hard that the trigger finger will not fully flex to pull the trigger. Another contributing factor is, when under sudden stress, a person's blood is drawn back into the main core of the body, in survival mode. When the blood leaves the extremities, you lose fine motor movement, and it is harder to use those extremities.

There are four things that could have changed the outcome in this situation. These things strengthened my belief in spiritual intervention.

1. I was carrying my Sig Sauer P220, a 45-caliber monster with a long, double-action first-trigger pull. I had a newly issued Glock in the back seat but was not scheduled to qualify with it for a few more days. If I had been using the Glock with the easy first-trigger pull, the weapon would have fired, and the driver would have died.

2. If the man had been driving, I am sure he would not have stopped, and both of us would have been seriously injured.

3. There had been a lot of burglaries in that area recently, so the vehicle was suspicious, and the officer just happened to check this street at that time.

4. Any other place on any other street would have allowed for more escape options.

Yes, they had just burglarized the home.

I don't know why this situation unfolded the way it did, but I have two theories. During the interviews the female driver asked, "Why did you pull that cannon on me?" My response was, "Why did you try to run over me?"

Theory A: Maybe I would not have dealt with taking a life as well as I thought I would. Even though I had mentally prepared myself for years, it is a possibility. If someone is involved in taking another person's life, even when justified, it can be difficult to work through. The aftereffects will drag on, since there may be criminal charges and investigations as well as civil liability in today's pay-me-now society. To work through this, I suggest seeking out assistance. Look for a peer-support team member if one is available. Seek out counseling with a therapist you trust. Listen to your attorneys when it comes to timing, as they may have you wait until the legal aspects of the case are resolved. But sometimes, you have to open up about the incident and how it has affected you so there are fewer lingering effects.

Theory B: I feel that this twenty-three-year-old woman had some purpose to fulfill, so it was not her time to go. Hopefully this scared her enough that she got away from her boyfriend and straightened her life out. I will never know for sure, but I believe this is the case.

———————

My wife and I traveled a bit since one of her daughters was a ski jumper, and we spent lots of time driving between SLC and Park City while shuttling kids to activities and events. We went to spin classes and rode bicycles together. That was actually when some of our best conversations took place. Riding bicycles together was enjoyable, and we had some great experiences. One time we rode the LaSalle Mountain Loop in Moab.

My wife continued displaying her anger and dislike of authority in statements she made about how she wished more cops would be killed and how they didn't deserve to be respected by the public. One of her favorite statements was that cops were just kids that had been picked on and bullied in high school and were only in their job because they wanted to have power now. These comments hurt and were hard to hear. I didn't deal with them. I just ignored them and tried not to respond. One day I came home and heard a loud bang in the basement. Then I heard it again. As I walked down the stairs, I heard a loud crash and turned to see my wife standing in the kitchen, looking at the tile floor. On the floor was a large, heavy, thick glass mug that my kids had given me when they were younger for making root beer floats. She simply said, "Damn, that was tough. It took me three times to break it." She was mad at me for something and broke it to get even with me. One of her most common statements in life was, "I don't get mad, I get even." She got even a lot, and most of the time I didn't even know what I had done. No one should condone or put up with this kind of behavior. I chose to stay, and it cost me dearly over the next few years.

I had my reasons. First, I was insecure and did not want to be divorced again—to be what I thought of as a "two-time loser." Second, my first wife had died, and I knew that losing another mother figure and moving out would really be hard on my son. I did not want to put him through that. Third, I had some sort of stability with my job, a place to live, and a life. Even though the relationship was unstable, the unknown outcome might have been worse. I now understand why abused women stay in relationships when they know they shouldn't. It doesn't make sense to stay, but we twist it in our mind, so it does. We do this out of fear. Again, not physical fear but fear of the unknown or fear of loss.

CHAPTER 21

THE RED DOOR

One day in a neighboring city, an angry husband who was a known gang member shot at his wife with a handgun. The woman fled to her parents' house in my city, and they called the police.

My sergeant and I were standing on the front porch talking with the family when the husband drove by. I ran out to my car to chase after him. I made a hurried U-turn and sped after the suspect. When I got to a stop sign, a block and a half from the house, I saw two cars. Both were the same make, model, and color. One was the suspect, the other wasn't, and I had no idea which was which. The front car turned left, going further into the subdivision, and the second car turned right toward the main road leaving the area. I followed the second car, activated my lights and siren and pulled it over. Once backup arrived, we pulled the occupants of the car out at gunpoint. It was the wrong car. It was a kid from California who had borrowed a car from friends in the neighborhood. I drove slowly back to the house, continuing to search the area for the suspect on the way. The family asked us to stay and protect their daughter. We offered to stay in the house, outside the daughter's room. However, the family had gang ties and did not want police in their home, so they declined that offer.

I was assigned to sit out front of the house in my car. I stayed there for several hours, but all I could see was the front door. Then I decided to move two houses up and across the street so I could see the front and one side of the house. About 0400 (4:00 a.m.) the girl's young brother came running out to my car yelling, "He is shooting everyone." I quickly ran from my car and charged through the half-open front door, weapon drawn, yelling into my radio, "Shots fired at the domestic house."

As I ran through the door, I saw three men fighting in the small living room. Mom and Dad were off to the left. I grabbed someone in the melee and pulled him away. One of the men had been knocked down to the ground. It was the suspect. I grabbed him and held him down while I cuffed him. I quickly looked around but could not see a gun anywhere. The other two men were brothers of the woman and had stayed over to protect her. Every time I would move away from the suspect, one of the brothers would punch or kick him. I finally pointed at one of them and told him, "You are in charge, make sure no one touches him. Every minute I have to spend protecting this jerk from you guys is a minute that I can't make sure your sister is okay. Got it?" He nodded.

I ran up the stairs and checked on the sister. She was lying on her back, in her bed, with a bullet hole in her forehead. A small trickle of blood oozed from the wound, down the bridge of her nose and onto her left cheek below her closed eye. She appeared dead. The suspect had parked his car three blocks away and sneaked through back yards to get to the house. He then sneaked in through a back window. He used a .22

handgun so the shots would not be heard outside the home. The victim was lying in bed with their two-year-old son cradled in her arms when she was shot. The child was not injured but had run out of the room. As the suspect had gone down the stairs to escape, the brothers had jumped him. I came back downstairs and was kneeling by the suspect when fire arrived. They came over to work on the suspect, but I told them that the victim was in the first bedroom on the right, just up the stairs. "You check on her first before you worry about this jerk," I said. Unfortunately, there was nothing that could be done for her.

By this time, everyone and their brother had arrived. Detectives and crime scene technicians took over, and I went outside to talk to the sergeant and just get away from the chaos. The gun was found in the living room on the floor against the front wall, hidden by some floor-length drapes. Sometime during the struggle, the suspect had also been shot near his right ear and later died. It was ruled a suicide.

AFTERMATH

About three months later I was dispatched to a possible DUI (driving under the influence) accident. There was a road that went westbound under the freeway. On the west side of the freeway, a narrow road went south then abruptly turned right after about 50 yards. That right turn had jersey barricades on its left side to keep vehicles on the roadway. As I approached, I saw a white Jeep CJ on top of the barricades. Not one wheel was touching the ground. As I stood there looking, the driver walked up to me. It was the father of the girl who had been murdered by her husband. He looked at me and yelled, "You, you're the one that killed my daughter!" I bit my tongue and didn't respond with any of the dozen things that came to mind. I was grateful that this location was half a block into the neighboring city, and I was able to turn the situation over to them.

The death of that young woman affected me a lot. I was at the scene to prevent it, but the family wouldn't let me in the home. I had been handicapped because I could only see the front of the house. And I know that if I had been inside, I would have been in a gun fight and stopped the guy. I was angry that this family hamstrung me from protecting their daughter and then blamed me. To this day I see the red front door of this home and the daughter's face with the bullet hole in her forehead, a small trickle of blood dripping down the left side of the bridge of her nose and onto her cheek. All the while she lay there on the bed looking like a fairytale princess, asleep, waiting for the kiss to wake her. When I think of it, I get chills, shake, and get tears in my eyes.

During this time, I built a spec home and made enough money to put a large down payment on a cabin. I also paid cash for a Harley. Little did I know that decision would be a factor in the end of my second marriage several years later. We rode with a group of friends during the summer and had a great time and some great experiences. During this time my wife's anti-authority, anti-police attitude really came out. She would say little in front of our friends, but when we were at home, I got it full bore. I had already begun shutting down in our relationship, and I shut down even more during this time. Her anger showed all the time, and she took it out on me.

I remember taking my son and leaving the house one night to avoid a fight. There was some event in town, and after checking four hotels I found no rooms and only one suite available. The price for the suite was so high that I would not pay it, so I had to go crawling back home. When I got there, I found many of the books from my library collection thrown out onto the front porch and front yard. I picked them up and put them back on the shelves in no particular order and went down to the basement to sleep on the couch. This was another emotional scar that I did not act on because of my fear. In addition to the problems described in the previous chapter, I trace some of it back to my fear of rejection and loss. I simply was not able to leave, because of fear. Fear of failure, fear of rejection, fear of loss.

CHAPTER 22

BETRAYAL

I started working part time for the transit police. They paid me the same hourly rate I made at Sandy PD, and I worked twenty hours a week on my days off. It was nice to finally have only one part-time job. Unlike other occupations, law enforcement has a lot of rules and requirements that remove many of our freedoms. I couldn't just go work any part-time job; I was required to get permission from the chief of police. I submitted my paperwork and was told by my captain (the former sergeant who had acted like a mentor to me) that I was good to go. And I did. This paperwork had to be renewed every year. At the end of the year, I resubmitted my paperwork. The captain approached me and asked me a strange question. "How long have you been working for transit?"

I gave him a puzzled look and responded, "For a year."

He looked at me and asked, "Without approval?"

The next day I was called into the chief's office and the questions were repeated.

Chief: How long have you been working for the transit police?"

Me: "For a year."

Chief: "Who gave you approval?"

Me: "I was told by the captain that you did and that I was good to go."

Chief: "Well, where is your paperwork?"

Me: "I don't know, I turned it in as required and assume it is in the file."

Big mistake. I did not keep a copy for myself.

Chief: "Well, it is not in the file, so I don't believe you turned it in. You've been working without approval."

Now my defenses were rising. Me: "I turned it in, and only lieutenants and above have access to that file, so I don't know what happened to it. And just a point: If I was hiding it, why would I turn in renewal paperwork this year?"

Chief: "Are you using any Sandy PD equipment when you work for transit?"

Me: "No sir. I have completely separate gear. I do wear the same boots occasionally."

Chief: "Okay, I don't want any liability issues. What would happen to you without that job?"

Me: "It's a third of my income, so I would be in financial trouble
        and possibly bankrupt in about six to eight months."

Chief: "Okay, I'll think about it."

Late in the afternoon of the next day, a Tuesday, the chief called me
in and told me I had to quit the transit job by Friday.

I told him that this wouldn't be fair to Transit since they had me
scheduled. I asked, "Isn't it professional courtesy and only fair to give
two weeks' notice?" He grudgingly agreed and gave me two weeks.

I was dismissed and went up the hall to the captain's office. I asked
him if he knew where the paperwork was, and he dodged the question.
"You may just have to quit that job. I was surprised when the chief
approved it anyway."

Me: "You know the chief approved it? Can't you remind him
         that he did?"

Captain: "No, I can't do that."

I recorded this conversation but didn't tell anyone (until now). I
violated policy recording this conversation, but they were messing with
my livelihood, which could have had a negative effect on my family.
Luckily, I never had to use the recording. But this was a big strike against
the captain for not standing up for his troops and the truth.

A couple of days later I was walking up the hall at the police
department when I was ordered into an office by two Lieutenants.
They had me sit down, then started grilling me about the paperwork.
They basically played good cop/bad cop while calling me a liar and
telling me to admit that I was lying about the paperwork. Their
problem was, I was telling the truth and there was no way I would lie
and say what they wanted me to. I even had the recording to prove it,

but that was my secret. I don't know if they were doing this on their own to prove themselves to the administration or if they were ordered to do this. I definitely learned who not to trust and what a hostile work environment was.

I notified Transit of the conversation but told them I still hoped to work things out. Then I spoke to an attorney. The next week I met with the chief in his office and brought my attorney, one of the best attorneys in Utah.

The chief was shocked and told me I didn't need an attorney. I told him, "Apparently I do. I did things right, turned in the proper paperwork, told the truth, and was discounted, called a liar, and punished for it. So yes, I need an attorney. The chief paused, looked at me, and said, "Well, okay. I will let you keep the job as long as you do things right. I'm not going to let anyone else work for another department though." I responded, "Thank you, sir, I appreciate it," and rose to leave. I was grateful for my attorney who stood up, looked at the chief, and asked, "And what about next year?" The chief slowly responded. "He can keep the job as long as he wants." He added, "I am going to have policy changed so this doesn't happen again, but you will be exempt."

As we left, my attorney gave the chief his card and said, "Good, I will look for this in writing at my office in the next couple of days."

I had not thought ahead to the future, but my attorney had. And that is why attorney's get paid the big bucks. It's also why I now have a department policy named after me. It is a running joke in police departments that you didn't have much of a career unless a policy was created to address something you did.

I worked for Transit for a couple more months before another sergeant's test was conducted. Again, I finished in the top five. Since the results for the top five candidates were posted alphabetically, the candidates often went around talking to each other, trying to figure out where exactly each had landed on the list. Part of it was curiosity. Part of it was to see who had an advantage. But mainly it was competitive. We were just trying to figure out who was best.

The closest I could figure, I was number three on this list, and the others agreed. This time there were going to be six or seven promotions. This was my fifth time placing in the top five candidates, so I felt good about my chances. Three sergeants were promoted first. All were senior officers like myself and good officers, but I was not one of them. Then three more were promoted. Candidates' numbers six and seven were promoted. Yes, my name was still on the list. I was not promoted. I had been left on the list for the fifth time in my career. Passed over for promotion for the thirteenth time.

I was mad, but I kept my mouth shut, put on a good face, and congratulated the new sergeants. Then I went to my mentor the captain and politely asked, for the sixth or seventh time, "What can I do better to make myself promotable?" He gave me an answer. It was completely different from any of his past answers, addressed nothing, and was obviously made up on the fly. I was suspicious now, and really felt I had been passed by because I stood up for myself and brought an attorney to deal with the previous issue.

I continued working at Transit, knowing there would be another promotion test in six months. A few weeks before the next sergeant's test, the captain pulled me aside and engaged me in a strange conversation. He asked how close I was to my twenty-year mark, and I told him I was less than a year away. Then he asked me if I had completed some federal work time before becoming an officer. He already knew I had, but I told him yes, six years. He said, "You know, you can use that federal time to buy out your retirement." I did not know that and had never thought about it. I just wanted to work, do my job, and be promoted when I deserved it. I felt I had earned the last promotion.

I looked into the federal time and found that I could use money from my 401K to buy out my retirement, but really didn't think much more about it. I spoke to Transit, and they said they would bring me straight over at the same rate of pay I was making at Sandy PD. I started seriously thinking about this option. *Wow,* I thought. *I could pull my retirement, fifty percent of my pay, the same as I make part time at Transit.* In other words, I could work forty hours a week, pull my retirement, and not lose any money. It sounded like a great idea to me.

The sergeant's test came, and to the dismay of the officers testing, I was not there. Rumors went around, and people started asking me why I didn't test. I simply shrugged. I thought about just walking away from the department without giving notice, like they had ordered me to do to Transit, but I knew that would not be professional. The day the new sergeants list came out, I gave my two-week's notice to the shock of many in the department.

I was really bitter at the department at this point. I still didn't know who I had angered to hold up my promotion. The only thing I could figure that made sense was that it was payback for bringing a lawyer and threatening to sue the department. I still couldn't figure out why the captain had suggested buying out my time and retiring. At the time, I hoped he knew something was in the works and was watching out for me. My wife said they were all "snakes in the grass, especially this chief and his administration Don't trust any of them." She was right. After I retired, I learned from friends who were lieutenants in the promotion meetings that for years the only one who spoke up against my promotion, every time, was my mentor the captain. Each time, he brought up my "magical mystery tour" that had occurred fifteen years before. Wow, I did not expect that. I now wonder if he did not put the paperwork into the file and was covering up for himself.

This just validated my wife's negative feelings about law enforcement and built up her arsenal of wrongs even more. She amped up her negative comments toward law enforcement and became even more angry.

It was interesting to compare work and marriage at this point. Both revolve around relationships, and both have good relationships and toxic relationships. I was now in a situation where my relationships at work were as toxic as my relationships at home. This was extremely stressful. I hung on to work, knowing I should have left years earlier. But out of loyalty to those who stood by me, I did not feel I could leave. After twenty years, I finally learned that it was okay to cut ties and move on, and I did. Unfortunately, I also knew I should cut ties at home, but I just couldn't bring myself to do it yet. Just like work, I hung on, hoping things would get better. I did the best I could to survive and work things out. At work, it only took one toxic person to stop the flow. At home, it was the same.

CHAPTER 23

TRANSIT

I retired from Sandy City Police Department in 2010 after nineteen years and three months and started working full time for the transit police. This was a pleasant change as I worked on the trains, busses, and property owned by the Transit Authority. This job was different because it was more customer-service oriented. I was excited about the chance to work in a new, growing department that might be a fresh start with new opportunities. I also wanted to get away from a negative situation; and for once I pulled the plug and moved rather than stubbornly staying, thinking I could pull out a win at the last second.

One day I was patrolling a parking lot in one of the train stations and saw a guy wandering around. He was looking in car windows and appeared to be checking cars. I stopped and talked to him. He gave me his identification information but did not have a driver's license or ID.

I did not have enough cause to hold him, so I allowed him to leave. Something didn't feel right, however, so when I got into my car, I looked up the information he had given me on my laptop computer. When that information came up, I realized he had lied to me. The description on the driver's license for the name and date of birth he had given me showed that he was 6'2" tall and 220 pounds with blond hair and blue eyes. The guy who gave me the information was 5'7" tall and maybe 160 pounds with brown hair and brown eyes. Knowing that people often use information they are familiar with, I checked the warrants list for someone with the same last name he had given me. There was one person with that last name who had $100,000 in felony warrants. I cross checked that name with the driver's license, and sure enough it was the guy I had been talking to. He had given me his brother's name and information.

I notified dispatch that I would be in the area, looking for the suspect. I drove across the street to the restaurant I had seen him enter. It had large glass windows all the way around, which allowed me to see the interior. He wasn't there. I recalled that while talking with me he had said he was looking for a phone to call someone for a ride. The nearest payphone I knew of was at a 7-Eleven store down the street. I drove there next.

I reached a stoplight facing west and stopped in the left turn lane. The freeway was in front of me. I could see the suspect in the 7-Eleven on the left corner. There was an island in the street, which forced me to make a U-turn to get to the 7-Eleven. I could have turned on my overhead lights to get through the intersection and traffic, but he would have seen that, run out the back, and been gone. Time drags so slowly when one is in a hurry. I was right by the freeway entrance/exit. Traffic was now exiting the freeway from the south while I waited. Next it exited the freeway from the north, and the seconds dragged by. Next the side street crossed north, then south, and then the cross streets left turn lanes. And still I waited. About this time the suspect, still at the 7-Eleven counter, saw me through the large glass window at the front of the store. I was acting as nonchalant as I could, so he didn't run as he exited the store.

My radio came on and someone asked, "Transit 34, do you have him yet?'

Without thinking, I responded, "I would if I could get through *swear word* traffic." I accidentally used a swear word on the air without thinking. During this time, I had seen the suspect exit the store. The traffic from the opposite direction was done, and finally it was my turn. I made the U-turn and pulled into the 7-Eleven parking lot but could not see the suspect. I got out of my car and looked. There was an alley to the side of the store with a ten-foot chain link fence and concertina wire on the top that blocked the end. He wasn't there. I could see through the store windows and noted he wasn't inside. I started walking around the parking lot, looking around and under cars and finally found him sitting on the ground, between two parked cars, trying to stay out of my sight. I ordered him out, and he decided he would rather fight than cooperate. After a brief struggle on the hood of a car and then onto the ground, I got him under control. As I was putting the cuffs on him, a shadow loomed over me. I finished handcuffing the suspect and I looked up. It was my chief. He grinned at me and said, "*swear word* traffic, huh." It wasn't good to swear on the radio, but the bad guy went to jail and that was all that was said.

This suspect had made a call, and about that time his father drove up. I was putting the suspect into the back seat of my patrol car when the father angrily stomped up and demanded, "What are you doing with my son?"

I replied over my shoulder, "He has warrants, and I'm taking him to jail."

The father yelled, "You can't do that, you're only Transit cops."

I clicked the lock on his son's seat belt, stood up straight, and moved directly in front of the father so I could look him in the eye. I glanced at the officer standing behind him, who grinned when I pointed at one word on my shoulder patch and asked, "What does that say?"

The father slowly answered, "Police."

I calmly responded, "Yes, it does, which means I can take your son to jail. When I get there, we will see who is right: you or me. By the way, you can probably visit him tomorrow at the jail."

And, yes, to the father's consternation, the jail took him.

It has always amazed me that criminals who don't want to deal with police will do stupid little things like not buying a ticket for the train— which means they end up dealing with police.

There was one big guy, around 6'4" and 260 to 280 pounds, who did not buy a ticket. I escorted him off the train and onto a service platform at one of the stations and was discussing the fact he had no ticket and had committed theft of service, a misdemeanor crime. The suspect claimed he did not have ID with him, which usually translated to, *I have warrants and am going to lie to you and give you false information and see if I can get away from you.*

Luckily, I had a good dispatcher who spotted a few of the lies he told me and figured it out while I dealt with the suspect. Yes, he did have felony warrants. Yes, he was a fugitive from corrections. Yes, he had assaulted an officer the night before and had escaped again. Now it was my turn. Statistics have shown that one of the most common times for a suspect to start fighting is at the beginning of being handcuffed. As I started to put the cuffs on this suspect, the fight started. My cuffs went flying, along with my sunglasses, cite book, personal cell phone, work cell phone, scanner, and anything else that was in a pocket and not tied down.

He jerked away from me and turned with his fists up. I used my taser for the first time in my career. The top prong struck him in the chest, as it was designed to do. The bottom prong however, bounced off his two-inch wide leather belt. If either prong does not connect, the taser does not work, and now the chase was on. He turned and ran. Since he was a big guy, I knew he wouldn't run far. I also knew I did not want to be in front of him to get pounded by those big paws or grabbed and mauled by those 260-plus pounds.

I jogged along behind him, formulating a plan. He started looking over his shoulder, and I knew the flight was over and the fight was coming. I figured that if I was on his back, he couldn't grab or hit me, so before he could turn around, I jumped on him. He went down to the ground and I went for the ride. I still had the taser in my hand, so I drive stunned him (placed the taser directly against the suspect's body) where his shoulder joined his neck. It didn't affect him, so I did it again. This time he turned his head and just glared at me. Now I was worried.

As we rolled on the ground, a truck driver pulled up at the curb in his semi and yelled "Are you okay?"

I responded, "I could use some help." He jumped out of his truck, grabbed one of the suspect's arms, and between the two of us we held the suspect down. My handcuffs were back on the train platform, so all we could do was hold the suspect down until backup officers arrived. A detective from the city we were in happened to be driving by, saw me fighting, and stopped to assist. We put that detective's cuffs on the suspect, but the suspect was so big that the cuffs would not reach both wrists. It seemed like an hour but was only a few minutes before another officer arrived. We hooked his pair of cuffs to the first pair, then to the other wrist, and finally had the suspect in custody.

Now I worried about all of my belongings and equipment that had been scattered on the train platform during the fight. I assisted the backup officer in putting the suspect into his car for transport and turned to go back to the train platform to find my things. At that moment, a homeless guy named Val walked up and held out all of my gear and equipment. He said, "People were taking your things, but I got them back for you. Here."

Val was an interesting guy. At one time, he was the director of maintenance over the largest school district in the country. He started having health problems, and his doctor told him he either had to quit working or he would die. He was forced to retire early, lost everything, and became homeless. Val hated the transit system so much; he would throw rocks at the trains as they passed. After several of these incidents, one of our guys took Val to lunch and talked to him with respect. I was not aware of that history, but when I met Val shortly after that I had treated him with respect. Because of that respect and connection, Val gathered all of my things and brought them to me.

———————

A couple of years later my wife and I got our first tattoos together. We also continued to ride my motorcycle with friends. She decided she wanted to ride her own bike, so we looked around and bought her a good starter bike, a Harley Sportster 1200. Unfortunately, this new bike was not good on the highway since it was too small and would be blown around and moved by the turbulence of passing trucks. We then shopped around more and traded it in for a larger road bike, a new Road King. This was my gift to her. Later, while we were still married, she went with her boyfriend and traded it in for a different bike. I didn't know he was a boyfriend at the time, but I was getting suspicious. He had full-body tattoos, and it wasn't long until she did also—some in very intimate areas. This was an additional clue that something suspicious was going on.

We went to Moab and spent time riding our motorcycles with our friends there. We had been touring around the area and staying in Moab.

On the third day, we were coming back from the Four Corners area when we saw a large red cloud of dirt and dust moving quickly toward us. When it hit, the wind blew my 1000-pound Harley with two riders on it three feet to the right. The red sand and dirt pelted us and cut visibility so that I could barely see in front of me. We slowed way down, and after a couple miles we were clear of that part of the approaching storm. This experience was reminiscent of my marriage. Lots of turmoil, lots of ups and downs, with lots of passion.

CHAPTER 24

SNAKE

I went to a sniper school during this time, even though I had never used a scoped rifle. I felt at the very least this would improve my skills and make me a better firearms instructor, especially when teaching patrol rifle. Little did I know it would become a lifelong passion.

The school was taught by the Utah County Sheriff's Department SWAT team and was very good. The course was conducted in Spanish Fork Canyon at the sheriff's department shooting range. This is a box canyon and is surrounded on three sides. The two sides on the right and left are mountains, and the end is a large hill with a small, rough road going to the top. The mountainsides drop down into a flat area where the main shooting ranges are located. There are several flat ranges varying from distances of twenty-five yards, to two hundred yards and are normally used for handgun or patrol rifle training. On the top of the hill at the end of the canyon is another shooting range that faces a draw on the mountain to the left. This allows precision shooters, snipers, to shoot out to 500 or 600 yards. I bought my own rifle, a Remington 700, .308 caliber, which was pretty standard in law enforcement at that time. It was matte black in color and set up with a Leupold Mark IV tactical scope, which was good equipment. We shot for four days, spending time setting up and adjusting our rifles, making sure we could sit behind our rifle without straining our necks and eyes and still see through the scope. We sighted in our rifles, shooting at one-inch circles at one hundred yards and shooting at various distances from twenty-five yards to five hundred yards. Students were developing skill and proficiency, even though the average law enforcement sniper shot was only seventy yards, we learned to observe details and report them while lying on the ground for extended periods of time. We also learned to be patient, since a sniper will likely be in one spot for several hours simply gathering information to assist in the decision-making processes during an operation. We were also introduced to camouflage and learned to conceal ourselves.

The last day and a half were the testing. There were several courses of fire, and the sniper candidates were required to pass each one.

One of the tests was "the stalk." On this day we were assigned a partner and an observer. The observer was an instructor who trailed along and observed as we went through the process. We put on our ghillie suits (a suit that is adapted to blend in with the surrounding terrain). After we painted our faces in a decent but amateurish manner, we were ready to go. We started on the top of the hill at the end of the range. The scenario was a hostage situation somewhere up on the mountain to the left. We were given limited information. If the "bad guys" (instructors) spotted us, we would have to hike back down the mountain and start again. There were some rolling meadows, with a gradual incline and waist-high grass, and we worked our way through those with ease.

We had only gone about a half a mile when the terrain changed. Now there was a sandy area with knee-deep reeds to the left and a slight hill to the right covered in scrub oak, with a tree here and there. We could hear some voices over the hill toward the front. We knew we weren't close, but sound carries in the mountains. It was a little warm, and both of us were sweating heavily in our ghillie suits. *Next time,* I told myself, *bring water.* We started crawling so we wouldn't be spotted. We crawled on our hands and knees another quarter mile, working our way up the mountain. I could see the next mountainside, dropping down on the other side of a ridge, and I knew there was a small valley there. The sound of talking voices lifted gently over the ridge. We didn't know how deep the valley was or if it was just a flattened area, so we sunk onto our stomachs and kept low crawling. I didn't want to start over. I was already tired. We chose to slide through the reeds and continued on our way, going slow so there would be no noticeable movement of the plants that might give away our location. My partner was just in front of me when he whispered excitedly, "Snake! Snake!"

About two feet in front of him was a three-foot-long rattlesnake, coiled but not rattling yet. *Please don't rattle. That will surely give us away. Please, don't strike.* The observer crept up behind us and quickly assessed the situation. He called out on his radio, and the targets agreed to turn their backs for thirty seconds to allow us to adjust our position and not get bit. We rose from the ground and started to move to our right in a crouch.

As we started to run, we saw four more rattlesnakes. We ran past them and got to the scrub oak-covered hillside, lowered ourselves to the ground, and resumed crawling. My partner got into a deadwood-protected circle and signaled me he had spotted the suspects. He signaled that they were about two hundred yards out. There was no room for me where he was and no way I could get a shot from there, so I belly crawled off to the right, looking for a place to shoot from. I saw a large patch of thistle and figured no one would look there for me. I crawled into the front edge and lay on my belly, prone on the ground.

I got the bipod (front support) on my rifle ready. I made sure the barrel of my rifle did not stick out of the thistle, since that would have been easily spotted by the instructors. I also made sure there were no branches or twigs in front of the barrel of my rifle. That would have deflected the bullet as it left the barrel, possibly causing me to miss the target. I lay there, my cheek on the butt of my rifle, looking through the scope, breathing deeply to recover from the exertion of our hike and crawl. I was about two hundred yards out.

The observer was near my partner, twenty yards to my left, when we notified him, we were in place and ready to shoot. I watched through my scope as the instructors/targets moved from the target area, leaving a head-sized, orange metal plate behind. I looked around, wondering where the other candidates were, and noted that we were looking into a bowl-type area with a ridge going around it on three sides. I was on the left side of that ridge. To my right I heard the boom of sound as someone pulled the trigger, and I watched as the bullet hit the metal plate with an audible ping. I could see the mark the bullet made on the metal. After four or five shots from the hillside to my right, I heard our observer tell my partner, "Take your shot." He did. The noise of the weapon was loud, and instantly there was a splat and a ping as the bullet struck the target. The observer came over to my area. "Williams, where are you?"

"Over here," I answered.

"Where?"

He was now about five yards from me.

"In the thistle."

"I can't see you, raise your arm."

I did, and he saw where I was.

"Okay, take your shot."

While lying there, listening to the bullets hit the target, I started to get a little excited. Now I breathed and thought things through. A cold shot, or the first round out of a gun barrel that day, hits in a different place then subsequent shots after the first bullet has warmed the barrel. I knew that at one hundred yards my cold shot would hit an inch and half low and to the left at the seven o'clock position. At two hundred yards, that would be three inches low and left. I settled in and snugged the stock of the rifle into the pocket of my shoulder. I looked at the target through my scope and focused the cross hairs of the scope at one o'clock, about three inches from the center of the target. I took a deep breath and exhaled slowly until my lungs were almost empty and the natural pause occurred. *Squeeze your finger slowly, be surprised when it goes bang.* The rifle moved against my shoulder as I gently squeezed the trigger. I maintained focus on the target, listening for the ping. The bullet struck just left of center.

The next day was my group's turn to be tested on the shooting range. I got to the last test without any retakes. The last test went as follows: take three shots, at the head of the target, from 200 yards, get up and run to a rickety, wooden table one hundred yards from the target. Use the wobbly table as support and complete three more headshots. Then run seventy-five yards and from a standing, unsupported position place three shots onto a body-sized target.

It was starting to get dark, and we were running out of time to get things done so everyone was hurrying. We had to do this test in two minutes or less. My name starts with a W, so I was the last to go. I completed my shots from two hundred yards and ran to the hundred-yard table feeding three rounds of ammunition into my rifle as I went. I completed my shots from the wobbly table and ran to the twenty-five-yard line, again, feeding three rounds of ammunition into my rifle. This time I got to the shooting line, aimed, pulled the trigger. Click, nothing happened. The magazine was not working properly. I pulled the bolt back to put another round into the rifle, and this caused my rifle to jam. I quickly stripped the ammunition out of the magazine and the rifle and put in one round of ammunition, aimed, and pulled the trigger. I repeated this process, hitting the target all three times. Unfortunately, my time was two minutes and three seconds, so I did not qualify. I was frustrated and mad. We were told we would get two attempts, but it was dark, and I did not get my makeup try. I went back home and worked with my rifle and scope. It was a small consolation, but one of the instructors told me, "If we had a most improved shooter award, you definitely would have received it."

I had some adjustments made to my rifle, and after a year of shooting and practicing I went back to another school. This time, I was a lot more confident and easily passed. The class was in the desert, and the stalk was a completely different experience. The rules were the same, but the terrain was flat, and the instructors could easily see us students if we weren't careful. My partner and I found a small canal ditch and were able to walk about a third of a mile toward the target in a crouched position. Then we found a small dip in the ground and began belly crawling for another half mile. It was hot, and once again I was dripping and soaked with sweat. I forgot to bring my Camelback and was getting dehydrated.

We could see the target (instructors) about two hundred yards away, on a small rise of ground. We crawled out of a low part of the meadow and positioned ourselves. My partner was behind a rock about the size of a child's tricycle, his rifle positioned on the right side. I was a few feet to the left, using the change in color from two types of wild meadow grass to conceal me. By this time, my partner and I were both cramping up. My calves and hamstrings were burning and almost useless. I was in pain as I shifted one leg and then the other, trying to relieve the cramps without giving our position away.

The observer called out and asked if we were ready to take our shots. My partner said he couldn't because he was cramped up. I told the observer, "Yes." I was hurting but was not passing up my reward. No cramps, pain, or anything else was going to stop me from getting my shot. I snugged the rifle into the hollow of my shoulder, looked through the scope, placed the crosshairs of the scope on the target, adjusted for the cold shot, and took a deep breath. I slowly let my breath out, paused, and slowly squeezed the trigger. The rifle moved against my shoulder. Ping, I hit the target and passed.

My second wife thought shooting was a waste of my time. This meant I did not go shooting as much as I should or would have liked. I was always looking out for what others wanted and penalizing myself. This might have easily been addressed if my wife and I had talked about it. Looking back in hindsight, I don't think it would have likely done any good, but at least I would have made an effort. I couldn't communicate at the time, especially about things that were important to me.

Sometimes we have to acknowledge that some problems can't be fixed. But I was so dead set on not being a failure in marriage again that I would not quit. This attitude probably stemmed from a combination of factors: Growing up, I was taught to never quit. I succeeded at many things because I kept on when others stopped, but my confidence had taken a beating over the years in law enforcement. Now, instead of standing up for basic decency and respect, I bottled things up and didn't even try. It just wasn't worth the trouble anymore.

My personal life and my career were curtailed because I gave up some of the things I enjoyed. Things that could have been beneficial to my advancement because I knew my wife did not agree with them. I've learned it isn't healthy to give up things you love. A healthy relationship may have areas where partners don't agree, but those partners will continue to support each other. This marriage did not have this dynamic and felt awfully one-sided. At this point in my second marriage, when we weren't at work, the only thing we talked about was taking care of the kids and getting them to their activities.

CHAPTER 25

INFECTIOUS

One day, I was assigned to work the trains in the University of Utah area. It was a late spring Saturday. Traffic was slower than normal, and as usual in Salt Lake City, it was quiet around this area. I was surprised to get a call from my sergeant, who informed me I would have a new partner for a few hours. The chief of police had requested to work with me. I thought that was pretty cool, but since this was normally a very quiet area, I thought he might be bored. It was boring as we checked tickets together on an eastbound train. We had written a few citations when I stopped a gentleman for not having a ticket. He was a thin, wiry male in his late twenties. He was rather angry and argumentative, not quite out of control but close.

It was common operating procedure to exit the trains with suspects, so we exited at a station on 400 South in Salt Lake City, one of the main roads leading from the downtown area to the University. The road was six lanes of constant, crowded traffic congestion. It was always busy, even on this quiet Saturday. I started talking to this gentleman, who surprisingly gave me his correct name. I was informed by dispatch that he had felony warrants, so an arrest was imminent. I informed him of this, and he immediately turned to run. The chief briefly caught ahold of the suspect's collar, slowing him down for a fraction of a second. That fraction of a second was all I needed. He crossed the rail lines next to the train platform, and I tackled him in the second eastbound lane in the middle of 400 South. The chief followed and landed on the suspect's legs. The suspect struggled and would not quit.

After several minutes we finally got him pinned down. I reached over the suspect's shoulder to grab his arm and position it behind his back so I could put handcuffs on. He leaned his head down toward my arm and snarled, "I have AIDS and I'm going to bite you." He put his mouth on my left forearm. I quickly jerked my arm away as he bit down. Suddenly, I remembered some old wrestling moves. I placed a forearm on the back of his neck and forced his head down onto the asphalt of the busy roadway. I reached under his arm, where he couldn't bite me, and plied his arm back until I had it behind his back. I put the handcuffs on that arm then cautiously worked his other arm back until I could get the cuffs on it as well. Then I leaned back, exhausted.

A normal fight on the street lasts for a minute or less. A long fight lasts for two or three minutes, and we had been rolling on the hot asphalt for ten minutes. As I lay back, four Salt Lake City PD cars pulled up. We asked the officers to place the suspect in one of their cars for us. My left calf was cramped, so I hobbled out of the middle of the street and sat on the curb to take care of myself. A little while later, the chief took me and some others to lunch. The cramp in my leg would not go away, and I was getting worried. I went to the doctor and learned that there was no cramp: One of the tendons in my leg, the one that held the top of my calf to the knee joint, had torn during the fight. I was on light duty for eight weeks while it healed.

As it turned out, the suspect really did have AIDS. He was charged with attempted aggravated assault on a police officer (assault with a deadly weapon) for trying to bite me and was sent back to prison.

I definitely talked to my wife about this experience. I had to go get a baseline test for AIDS since his mouth had been on my arm. There were teeth marks, but no skin had been broken as I jerked my arm away. I had to get tested every three months for a year, but it turned out okay. My wife was worried and justifiably so. We didn't have much physical contact for a while until tests came back clear. I was sure I had not been contaminated but decided that it was better to be safe than sorry. This was extremely stressful at the time. We talked about it, laid down safeguards for not contaminating my wife, and went back to our normal routine. We just did not have sex.

Despite our relationship problems, my wife was very good with my son. I remember fighting with him to get him to graduate from high school. After his mother, my first wife, died I worked like crazy to get him interested in things. He was struggling in school even though he was a smart kid. I did everything I could to help him learn to do his work and get decent grades. I rewarded him, punished him, helped him with homework, and anything else I could do to get him to work at it. One time in junior high, I went with him to a parent-teacher conference. When the first three teachers informed me that he was failing, I was stunned and asked how that could be. They told me he had not turned in any homework. Now I was mad. I had done the homework with him and knew he had done it. I marched him out of the room and demanded to know where his homework was. He took me to his locker and opened it up. There was a thick, crumpled stack of papers on the bottom of his locker. We sat there on the floor and sorted the missing homework by class. I told him we were taking it to his teachers. He said, "But Dad, they won't give me credit now."

I sharply retorted, "I don't care. At least they will know you did it, and you will know that you completed the assignment by turning it in."

A few years later, after graduating from high school, my son entered the military and joined the Army. I went to his graduation from Advanced Infantry Training. He did so well that he was sent directly to the 82nd Airborne. After graduation he pulled me aside and in a very mature way said, "Dad, thank you. Sometimes you were a hard on me, and I hated you when I was a kid."

I looked down at the ground and quietly replied, "I know."

Before I could say more, he interrupted and continued. "But you taught me to never quit and to finish things, and that is why I did so well. I love you. Thank you for putting up with me."

A couple of years later, I received an early morning phone call that really shook me to the core. I had taken the day off work and was sound asleep. At 0600 hours (6:00 a.m.) my cell phone rang, waking me from a deep sleep. My first thought was, *Come on, Sarge. I took the day off.* But when I picked up the phone, it was my son. He was in Afghanistan. We had been emailing for eight months, and I was surprised to hear his voice. In our emails, he had told me of all of the things he was doing and about several close calls fighting the Taliban. Each fight seemed worse than the one before. We always started our emails with the bad news and ended with the good, because that was what we wanted to concentrate on.

His voice on the other end of the phone said, "Hey Dad, I've got good news."

Me: "What is that?"

Alex: "I'm coming home."

I knew something was wrong and could only ask quietly, "How bad is it?"

He had been on his last mission before coming home, and a buddy of his had stepped on an IED next to him. After he got home, Alex spent over two years in the military hospitals and had thirty-five surgeries to repair the damage. His life as a physically fit twenty-year-old young man had been altered drastically. My wife was a great support for him and me during this time. She always was when it came to the kids.

My son and I didn't really talk about stress and PTSD, but I soon saw some of the results of his own struggles with trauma. We went on a tour for wounded warriors to Gettysburg battleground. The last stop on the tour was a diorama of the three-day battle. The lights went low, and there was such a sudden unexpected uproar of explosions that I jumped, hurriedly ducked, and looked around. That was nothing compared to my son's reaction. He slid down as far as he could in his motorized wheelchair, using it for cover. He was peeking around the back of the chair, looking for the enemy.

After that, we started talking about PTSD a little. The military hospitals were set up to address this issue since it was nothing out of the norm for these returning soldiers. My son was in individual counseling as well as group meetings. People brought comfort dogs around the wards for the soldiers to interact with. For months, my son blamed himself for the IED. On the trek out, he had marked the IEDs with a red ribbon as he had been trained. Now he wondered if he had done it correctly or had used the wrong color ribbon. Was he to blame, somehow, for his friend's misstep? It took a while and a lot of counseling for him to finally admit he was not to blame. He had followed procedure and done things correctly. This is an example of the human fallacy of blaming ourselves for events out of our control. My son still suffers from PTSD today and absolutely hates the Fourth of July holiday because of his reactions to the surrounding fireworks. He is aware of what happens and prepares himself each year by speaking with the neighbors about it and asking them if they will move down the street with their fireworks. Sometimes he goes out into the mountains where there is no surrounding barrage of explosions; this is just one way he copes with his PTSD.

CHAPTER 26

ARMED AND DANGEROUS

Once again, I stopped a gentleman who had no fare to be on the train. And once again, we exited onto a station platform. He gave me his personal information without ID, and the information did not match anyone in the statewide system. I had a feeling this was someone with a serious past, so my partner kept a close eye on him as I stepped to the side to figure out the truth with dispatch. After a few minutes, we found an ID that matched him. He had reversed the month and day on his date of birth when he gave me his information. The new, correct information included a warrant by the US Marshals Service for running guns and drugs. I immediately put him at gunpoint, and we took him into custody. He immediately told me, "You've got the wrong guy, I've had this happen before," and tried to persuade me I was wrong. He even said, "Don't get nervous Barney, you're scaring me," in an attempt

165

to dissuade me. The good news was that scars, marks, and tattoos don't lie. I had dispatch send me a photo. It looked like him but was a poor-quality photo. However, the tattoo on his neck in the photo matched the one we saw in real life and removed all doubt.

The marshals wanted this suspect so badly that they would not let me take him to jail. I had to drive to the Federal courthouse in Salt Lake City and turn him over directly to the Marshals Service. When I got to the detention area of the Federal courthouse, I opened the rear car door to get the suspect out. As I did, I saw several baggies of white powder on the floor of the car between the suspect's seat and the door. They later tested positive for methamphetamine. The suspect looked at me and said, "Those aren't mine."

I laughed and told him, "Yes, they are. I search my car after every prisoner, and they weren't there when I put you into the car. I know they aren't mine." I turned him over to the US Marshals Service, and we added possession of methamphetamine with intent to distribute to the already lengthy list of charges.

———————

One Christmas Eve, my wife and I were home with the kids. My son had a couple of friends over. Apparently, his friends weren't going to have much of a Christmas at home, and my son asked if they could stay over. We said yes, but that upset one of his stepsisters who had OCD (obsessive compulsive disorder). She was bothered that we didn't have any presents for them and that it wasn't planned. She got angry and threw a fit.

I went upstairs to our room and sat in a chair in the corner of the bedroom. My wife came up stairs and began angrily stalking back and forth, ranting about the situation and her daughter's attitude. She went to her dresser and pulled out her handgun, saying, "I should just use this and put me out of my misery," as she put the weapon to the side of her head. "I should shoot [her daughter] too. What kind of life is she going to have as an OCD drug addict anyway?" After what seemed like an eternity but was only a few minutes, she stormed off to the walk-in closet. Then she started yelling, "Where's the clip? Where's the clip to your gun?" I knew her weapon was loaded, but my duty weapon was in the closet on the shelf unloaded, since I was getting ready to clean it. The magazine (clip) was next to the weapon on the shelf, but she was so angry she didn't see it. Something told me to stay in the chair, but I didn't listen. I got up and walked into the closet. She was standing there with her loaded stainless steel 40 caliber Sig Sauer in her right hand and my unloaded black Glock in her left. As I walked into the closet she yelled again, "Where is the clip to your gun?' I could see it where I had put it, on the shelf about a foot and a half to her right. I walked closer and said as calmly as I could (which probably didn't sound very calm), "Just put the guns down."

As I walked closer, she raised the loaded gun in her right hand and pointed at my chest. I was close enough that she pushed the gun forward into my chest. I felt the muzzle slide off my sternum, over a rib, and into the notch between the next rib on the left side of my chest as she again demanded the clip to my duty weapon. I raised my hands about shoulder height. I was now basically, a hostage. I started talking to get her to put the weapon down. The next few seconds felt like an eternity as thoughts also flashed through my head about what I had been taught about how to take a weapon away in martial arts:

I considered method one, then dismissed it. *No, I can't do that since the weapon often discharges to the right, in the direction some of the kids were.*

I considered method two, but no. *The weapon often discharges down into the floor in the direction of our daughter's bedroom below us. I knew she was in there.*

I rejected method three. *No, the weapon will discharge into the chest of the person with the weapon (my wife). I am not killing my wife or any of the kids.*

At that moment my wife raised the weapon. The muzzle crossed my chest and came up until it was a couple of inches from the right side of my face and ear. Then *boom,* she pulled the trigger. The bullet struck the ceiling a few feet behind me. I reacted, and as she lowered the weapon back to my chest. I hit my wife in the jaw with my right hand, knocking her down. She dropped my empty duty weapon against the wall to her left, my right. Her loaded weapon still hung limply in her right hand as she slumped to the floor. I took it from her hand and tossed it among some shoes on the floor to her right.

My wife struggled groggily to her feet with a glazed look in her eyes. I helped her into the bedroom and sat her on the edge of the bed. One of her daughters who had heard the boom of the .40 caliber weapon came running in. My wife could barely talk or move her jaw, so we went to the hospital. Her jaw was broken in three places and had to be wired shut.

The next day I made a mistake that negatively affected both of us. I knew I had to get out of the house immediately, so I called a friend I worked with at the police department and asked him if I could store my Harley at his place. I also told him what had happened and asked him to keep this to himself. He agreed, but then he called our lieutenant and told him what had happened. The lieutenant called the local police, and when I got back from the hospital, they were waiting at the house for me. Against my wishes, they went to the hospital to question my wife. She asked if she needed an attorney while she was being prepped for surgery and on medications, and still they insisted on questioning her. My wife was charged with aggravated assault, a second-degree felony. I was disciplined at work for not reporting a crime and not storing my weapon properly. These policy violations cost me a chance at the next promotion test, since the department would not let me test, while being disciplined.

I spent the next two years trying to repair this marriage and going to court with my wife. I stood up for her, and she got the case pled down to a misdemeanor. It still affected her work, since her security clearance was revoked, and she couldn't work on some government projects that she had. She didn't think it was fair that she got a broken jaw, criminal charge, and had to go to anger management classes while nothing happened to me. She blamed that on cops taking care of each other and said the only reason nothing happened to me was because I was a cop. Little did she know the difficulties I went through at work for the next year. Being removed from the promotion process was only the beginning.

At this point my wife and I were separated, and I lived at the cabin. I had to get up at 0300 (3:00 a.m.) every morning and drive fifty-seven miles to work. I was still trying to rebuild the marriage, and my wife agreed to me coming down to Salt Lake for a weekly date. I looked forward to our weekly dates and really tried to make things work for the next two years but didn't succeed. I didn't find out until later that she had already moved on. She already had had a boyfriend for quite a while. For most of our marriage, communication was an issue and usually turned into jabs and sarcasm. In the end, we just didn't talk. We didn't do anything together, and I was replaced emotionally and physically by a guy she worked with; the guy who rode motorcycles and had a body full of tattoos.

During this time, my wife went through some personal growth training called Impact trainings. The change in her was dramatic, and the constant anger seemed to be gone. It was such a positive change that I wanted it too. I went in and signed up for the training. During the first training called Quest, I participated in exercises and processes in small and large group settings. During these exercises I was introduced to the way I have been living my life. How I took things for granted, which created situations where I didn't follow through or didn't do what I said I would because I was so focused on myself. I learned to look inside myself and take accountability so I could look outside of myself and be of service and grow. I learned to stand by my word, no matter how insignificant it seemed.

I saw the fixed beliefs and walls that I had, many of which I was unaware. I started to trust myself and get rid of the manipulation games I played and saw so often around me. I grew and was no longer afraid to let people see the real me. I realized I was not deficient because of who I was, what I had seen, or what I had done.

I also learned to communicate simply, openly, and honestly. To get rid of ambiguity and to just be in the moment, right here, right now. I knew but hadn't accepted that one of my strengths was teaching and training. In a nutshell, I regained the real me that I had hidden away for so many years. Participating in this training turned out to be the most significant choice in my life.

KILL A COP

I was checking fares on the south part of the train system on a northbound train when I found a man who had no ticket. I did not know that he had purposely chosen not to purchase a ticket, hoping he would be stopped by the police. This man did not appear to pose a threat, so my patrol partner went to the next train car to check fares there. I was alone, at least until the next station. As I was talking to the man, explaining his violation and citation, he said, "You're way too nice, you're making this hard."

"Making what hard?" I asked

He repeated, "You're being too nice."

"What's going on?" I queried.

He calmly and coolly told me, "I was going to kill a cop today and hopefully die doing it, but you are making it difficult."

The hair on the back of my neck stood up. Anticipating a physical confrontation, I asked, "And how were you going to do that?"

He responded, "I have a knife in my coat pocket."

I called on the radio for backup, knowing there would be none until we reached the next station.

I told him, "I'm going to move behind you and take the knife. Please don't reach for your pocket because I do not want to have to hurt you."

I moved behind the man and removed a lethally sharp butcher knife with a six-inch blade from his right-side jacket pocket. As I stowed the knife safely in the cargo pocket of my pants, he said, "I have a screwdriver in my other pocket."

I then took a large, sharpened straight-blade screwdriver out of the left side jacket pocket and placed it in my same pocket. By that time, my partner was back, and we placed handcuffs on the man and exited the train at the next station.

We learned that this man had not been taking his medications. We also learned that he had been hoping to run into one of our newer officers, who had been forceful and authoritative with him a couple of days before. He was mad and was willing to take on any officer he came in contact with. Our personal actions and behaviors, good or bad, can have an effect on other officers and other people's lives. The officer this man was looking for was only two stations away from where we got off the train.

I called an ambulance, and instead of a citation or jail I had him transported to the psychological unit for evaluation. About two years later, this same man approached my lieutenant on a train and asked him to thank me for saving his life. He had gone to Arizona for inpatient treatment for a year, was back on his medications, and had moved back to Salt Lake City. He had a good job and was doing very well.

———————

I had been learning to be open, nonjudgmental, and to communicate better. These skills paid off when I chose not to fight. This experience was unlike so many others in the past. Being open and sincere and letting him see I cared kept this man from attacking me.

For the first time in many years my wife and I had an open honest conversation. This was only possible for me because of the things I had learned. She sincerely told me she just wasn't cut out to be partnered with only one person (married). I knew that was not the type of life I wanted to live and expressed that. We mutually started working on a divorce. We got a mediator, and a short time later it was done. I wasn't happy since it cost me more than I felt it should have, but now I was divorced again. In my mind I was a two-time loser. I was still being hard on myself. It would have been easy to blame everything on my wife, and the old me would have done that. Instead, I took an accountable look at what I had contributed to the failure of the marriage and recognized that I had quit talking again. I had shut down and built walls. I had been defensive. I had contributed tremendously to this failure. Still, even though I needed to take responsibility for my own actions, I couldn't change her behavior or choices and finally knew it wasn't going to work. I am grateful to my former wife for being such a good stepmother to my son and for introducing me to Impact training, which has been such a positive influence in my life. I still go to training and work on the inner parts of me and the spiritual aspects of my life.

CHAPTER 28

DOCTOR DEATH

One unpleasant part of my job was responding to and investigating train/pedestrian and train/vehicle accidents. It always bothered me when the news would report these incidents as a train hitting a car, rather than accurately stating the fact that a car drove in front of the train, or a person walked in front of a train. A train cannot stop or swerve to avoid an accident.

One eight-week stretch on the job earned me the nickname "Doctor Death." It seemed that every time I went to work, someone walked in front of a train. There were four train/pedestrian accidents during that period of time, and each one of them happened on my shift and in the area I was covering that day.

One day a teenage girl and a couple of her cousins were walking home. The young girl was not looking where she was going, distracted by the conversation with her friends, and possibly wearing stereo earbuds. She stepped out and never saw or heard the train as it rapidly approached. The train operator was in a lose/lose situation. He hit the emergency brakes, but there was no way the train could be stopped in that distance. He sat there, sliding along the rails, knowing the girl would be hit. He knew he would have a front row seat to the carnage since she would strike the front of the train a foot or two in front of him, and he would have a clear, detailed view through the thick front windshield glass.

I arrived, and the scene was not pleasant. The girl's body had been thrown out of the railway across two traffic lanes and a sidewalk and lay lifeless against the curb of the center median of the road. She was twisted like a mistreated doll, legs here and arms there, but at unnatural angles. Of course, there was blood. And then there were the cousins and the onlookers, and someone would have to tell the family. I had to control the scene first, deal with the witnesses and collect the evidence second, then notify the family.

This incident made the national news and forced changes in train crossings. The crossings now have zig-zag railings that force a person to look up to avoid hitting a railing as they turn right and left, back and forth. This draws their attention to the rails and any oncoming trains.

The second incident occurred on a frigid morning with white frost on the ground. I got to work and immediately got a call from Sandy Police about a body that had been found on the rails in their city. It was a woman in her mid-twenties who had been struck by a train. The trains were just beginning to run for the day, so this must have occurred late the previous night when freight trains leased the rails.

The girl had been partying at a house nearby, which was in a residential circle across the street from the tracks. She had left the party, but friends at the party were fuzzy on the details. She left around 0100 (1:00 a.m.), and that was the last time she had been seen. The girl apparently climbed through the barbed wire fence bordering the tracks and was walking on the tracks in the pitch-black night. There was no lighting. The dark night combined with the dark clothes the girl was wearing made it impossible to see her.

There was some speculation by her friends that she may have stepped in front of the train on purpose, but as far as I know that theory has never been proved or disproved. Either way, when I arrived, I found another mangled corpse. The damage that a 100,000-pound train car, multiplied by three, does to a human body is horrific. Thankfully, there was no crowd this time. I gathered evidence and photographed the scene. In this case, there was a bigger scene since the body was in several parts. I covered the body and bloody body parts while I waited for transport. Then I identified her and notified her family.

Incident number three happened when a middle-aged man parked his car at the curb next to a rail crossing. This was a quiet road with very little traffic, so no one would notice him. He sat in the car and waited, looking at his watch. When it was time, he opened the driver's side car door and looked around. No one there. Good. He left the note he had written on the driver's seat of the modest, worn sedan. Video from a nearby business showed him as he stretched and straightened his body then looked up the rails to the north. His meeting with destiny would be coming at any moment, and he walked steadily toward the railroad tracks. He stood there, trying to appear casual as if waiting to cross the lines. The crossing arms began to flash and ring, and he knew it was time. From inside the crossing arms, he stepped out into the rails, timing it so that the train could not stop in time to avoid this meeting. He had decided he was done struggling with the feelings he was having and the things that were happening in his world. He was done with life.

Once again, a human body was struck by the front end of a 400,000-pound train, mangled, caught and dragged on the undercarriage, smearing blood along the way and leaving a grotesque red mural on the ground. Luckily there were no bystanders, but the incident was caught on the surveillance video of a nearby business. I had to photograph, measure, document, gather the evidence, and cover the body out of respect. I found the car keys in his pocket. Called the family.

Did we need a wrecker for the car? Why would someone do this? Were things that bad? What made him decide to do this? So many questions that may never be answered.

I responded to these calls and many others. Part of the job is to investigate, document, and report what happened. This entails inspecting, measuring, photographing, and maybe diagramming the scene. Protecting the public by covering the victims. Part of the job is seeing body parts, blood, and all manner of things that can have a detrimental effect on the human psyche.

———————

I was so tired of dealing with these accidents. It was humorous to be called Dr. Death but not to live it. I wanted it to stop. I hurt for the families and was tired of dealing with the hurt and anguish caused by these thoughtless acts or oblivious accidents. I didn't want to see the blood or twisted bodies anymore. I didn't realize this at the time, since I simply went into work mode and ignored the pain. I blocked out what I saw. Once I wrote the details of the accident down on paper in my report, it was gone—or so I thought. I now know that is not the case, because I still can envision each and every incident. I very rarely do so, since the view is not what I want to see, and I do not want to feel the pain that is left behind for law enforcement and the families to deal with.

I was living alone at the cabin during this time. My divorce was not final, and I had no one to talk to outside of work. I was seeing a counselor to deal with my divorce and the action of hitting my wife. I was taught from boyhood that a man was never supposed to hit a woman, and I was beating myself up mercilessly even though the blow had been in self-defense.

The isolated cabin in the midst of the aspen trees had always been my weekend getaway. It was my retreat, my sanity break in the peaceful quiet with the aspen trees whispering in the breeze, the shade, and cool mountain air away from the heat of the summer in the valleys below. It had always been a place of inspiration for me.

Now the cabin felt like a prison. The life I thought I wanted had been pulled out from under me. It wasn't my choice, and now I had no other option. I was forced to be here all the time, but it was definitely better than the rundown apartment I lived in after my first divorce.

I felt trapped in my life at the cabin, in the carnage I saw at work, and the political games from dishonest, unethical people. So, I started to drink. First, it was once or twice a week or when watching sports. Then it was every night when I got home from work. It was only two drinks a night, but they were thirty-two ounces each. I was never really drunk, but I no longer felt the pain. The emotional pain from feeling betrayed in my relationship. The pain from seeing bloody body parts and dealing with death, and the pain of loss for the families. Physical pain from the bumps and bruises of foot chases and fights at work, or from shoveling piles of snow up to eight feet deep. *Oh brother,* I thought. *I'm not young anymore.*

It didn't matter. For a few hours, those pains were gone and being alone in the cabin was no longer a prison as life was numbed by the slow creeping, mind-numbing warmth of alcohol. I did this for several months then realized I didn't like where I was heading or the way I felt. I had already lost one stepbrother to alcohol. He died in his mid-forties because of complications from addiction and overuse. I did not want to follow that path and knew I couldn't sit up at the cabin alone any longer.

I signed up for a local gym, and even in bad weather I would stop there on the way home from work. I started working out, which took my mind off being alone. I started working around the house again and found little projects to work on. I started keeping myself busy. I still did not have a social life, but I started searching out things to do. Snowshoe, go to the gym, ride my bike inside on a stationary stand, reload ammunition, go to the coffee shop and meet someone new, anything to not be home alone with nothing to do. I cut back and no longer drank every night. It was my choice, and I made the choice to do something useful. If you cannot do this, find a support group to assist you. I have attended AA meetings and other dependence groups with friends and family, and they were always helpful and made a difference in the lives of those who were there.

These behaviors are not uncommon for people with PTSD who are dealing with stress. Many turn to addictive substances such as alcohol or drugs. Others turn to healthier behaviors like exercise: running, cycling, or weightlifting. All have their downsides, but some are healthier than others. In my case, I was eight miles from town and my time was limited. I didn't want to do the extra driving to the gym, so once I got home, I turned to the easy thing: Pour a drink and forget about life. Studies have shown that PTSD will affect about eight people out of one hundred in the United States. The numbers are much higher in the public safety sector. Statistics show that approximately sixty percent of those who suffer from PTSD will also battle addiction problems.

CHAPTER 29

THE LAST HURRAH

During this time when my relationship at home was destroyed, my work was affected as well. I was preoccupied with saving my marriage. The fact that I ended my friendship with some people at work as I remade my life also created problems. I discovered who my real friends were and thinned the crop, removing those who were not.

I was on a specialized team, and we dealt with specific problems throughout the transit system. I made some small mistakes in reports, and suddenly it felt like I was back in my original field training. I would fix one purported problem only to have another one brought up. I would fix that problem, and something else would be brought up. I was a twenty-five-year officer who had never had these problems. This was my third sergeant at UTA, and none of the others had problems with my reports. I was verbally warned one week, given a written warning a few days later, and the next week I was put on a year's probation for having report writing problems. I was removed from the specialized team, removed from my position as a firearms instructor and all other specialty jobs, and sent back to patrol. I went from being one of the top three officers in the department for the past three years to being on probation.

My department got a new chief, and when he found out about this, he was dumbfounded that I had been put on a year's probation for report writing. He looked at my reports and said, "This is minor. And you got put on a year's probation for this?" The new chief reinstated me to my former positions and ended the probation; however, I still take accountability for worrying about my marriage and being distracted from my work.

When I went through personal enhancement training, I learned that I was accountable for what I had contributed to the downfall of not only my work but my marriages. In both cases, I quit talking and communicating. I quit trying in the first marriage. In the second marriage, I went into survival mode and did not relate emotionally. If I couldn't talk about anything other than surface-level topics, is it any wonder she went somewhere else for fulfillment.

I went to counseling, and over a year's time I dealt with the feelings of inadequacy I felt. I traced these feelings back to incidents like, that day as a twelve-year-old at the ballpark with my father. I dealt with the fact I hit my wife when she fired the weapon and I reacted defensively to take it away. I realized I wasn't just a cop, and being a cop wasn't my life. I worked as a police officer to make a living, and for the first time in many years I saw and felt the difference. Once I started going to personal enhancement training, I didn't stop until I had taken every training level I could. After the training, I went back to my therapist/counselor. We met, and after our meeting she told me, "You are good, you don't need me anymore." During the training, I worked through things that had been traumatic or detrimental to me, and afterward they no longer bothered me. Now I could talk about anything openly, without judgement. I no longer beat myself up in regret of things that had happened, or things I had done.

During this time period I was still up at the cabin, and I had to shovel a lot of snow in the winter. I had fallen and injured my shoulder, and I had to have rotator cuff surgery to repair it. One day, there was about a foot of new snow. I was still in a sling and not supposed to move my shoulder, but I had to shovel the snow to get out. I could have called my son but did not want him to drive sixty miles through bad weather to help me, so I shoveled with one arm. I was sore later, but this showed me that the stubborn, I-can-do-this-on-my-own attitude was still there. I got the stubborn streak early in life. Sometimes it got me through, but I still had a lot to learn—like that it's okay to ask for assistance.

Over the following year, several other things assisted me in surviving my law enforcement career. I took to heart the advice given in the academy of getting a hobby outside of law enforcement and continued teaching scuba diving, becoming one of the top instructors in the state. This was peaceful, enjoyable, and a release. I enjoyed working with people and rarely thought about work when I was teaching. It got me out of the city on my weekends off and broadened my horizons as I went to the Caribbean Islands, Hawaii, Mexico, and places I had only dreamed of going to.

I started taking martial arts as well, at first thinking it would give me an advantage if I got into a fight at work. That thought soon disappeared as I learned more about the art and the beliefs behind it. I worked hard over the years, and the physical release of a hard workout was definitely a bonus. I improved my discipline while learning martial art forms and finding the time to practice accordingly. When I got divorced the first time, I stopped practicing martial arts for a couple of years. Then I missed it and went back. I have worked hard to achieve my second-degree black belt, and even though I have moved away I still Skype with my instructor to keep up, and I train when I am in town. Learning martial arts gave me a physical release and taught me discipline and how to think under pressure. How to be at peace, yet able to respond to any action.

I was still married to my second wife, but the divorce process was almost completed. Now that I knew that relationship was over, I felt free to start dating again.

I started online dating, which was a big risk for me since I didn't use computers much outside of work. I met eleven women online and went out with nine in about ten days until I was physically exhausted, and out of money. They were all very nice, but something was missing in each one. I now knew what I wanted or didn't want in a woman.

I started talking to the tenth woman. We talked on the phone every night for hours. We talked and talked and have never stopped. Unlike most of the others, who wanted to go out then maybe get to know me, we got to know each other first by talking. For the first time in a long time, I actually talked openly about my experiences and how I felt about them. I allowed her to look past the surface, past the protective barriers I had put in place as a "cop" and let her see me. Not Glen the cop, or Glen the scuba instructor. Those were things I did, not who I was. I let her see Glen who loved his kids, who celebrated their achievements with a BBQ, who loved martial arts and being active. Glen who had written a program to assist other officers. I let her see the spiritual, healing, loving Glen. I opened up and in turn looked deeper into her and saw a woman who loved life and her kids. A woman whose job was directing/managing an art gallery in Park City. A woman who cared for humanity, who lived to give service to others, who had started a nonprofit to provide educational opportunities for the deaf. And this was just the surface.

I drove fifty-seven miles to work every day and was scheduled for work at 0600 hours (6:00 a.m.). This means I got up at 3:00 a.m. to get ready, get my uniform and gear put together, and go. This woman and I were talking one night, and she asked me, "Don't you have to work tomorrow?"

"Yes," I replied. "Why?"

She responded, "Well, it's one o'clock. You probably should get some sleep."

The time had flown. I had no idea it was that late.

I went to a family reunion in another state for a few days, and we continued to talk several times a day. It got to the point that I would be on the phone and my kids or siblings would say, "Oh, are you talking to _____ again?" I just laughed, and now they see why.

We scheduled a date. It was nice to finally be open and honest and not judged, and to talk with someone who was open and honest too. I realized I had held back in my other relationships out of fear. Fear of judgment, fear of saying or doing the wrong thing, fear of letting someone down or disappointing someone. Because of the training I went through, I no longer had those fears. She recognized that and loved that about me, and I recognized the same things in her and loved that.

We talked for about two or three weeks, then scheduled our first date on a Friday evening. I was in town on the Wednesday before and called her. I told her, "Hey, I'm in town and really don't want to wait until Friday to meet you. If you're not busy, would you meet me tonight?"

She told me she was busy for about half an hour but would love to meet me. We met at an outdoor patio restaurant. While waiting for her I ran into the old city prosecutor from Sandy City, who had just retired. We chatted and then parted ways. A few minutes later she arrived. It was like we had known each other forever. She was and is loving and gentle, looking for the positive in everyone and every situation. The bond we started while talking was strengthened. I found out later that she was getting a manicure when I called and had hurried up to finish so she could come see me. We went on our first official date that Friday in Park City to a sushi restaurant. We were sitting down to eat, and who should walk by? It was the same prosecutor from a couple of days earlier. I started to introduce my date and went totally blank on her name. "Donna" came to mind and I knew that wasn't it. After hemming and hawing for a few seconds, she graciously stepped in and introduced herself. Later I laughed and said, "at least I had the first letter correct." She started calling me Gary and any other name she could think of that started with a G. We laughed about it then and still do. I knew she was a keeper, and we have never been apart since. We have a phenomenal life.

The first year we were together, we moved four times. She had a house in the city but felt it was too much work, so she had put it up for sale a few days before we met and bought a condo. I had to have a second surgery on my shoulder to get it to move better. I would come home from work, and she would have me lie on the floor and tell her stories of my life and things that had happened at work that day while she moved my arm through my physical therapy exercises. This is one of my favorite memories.

Two days before we met, I had bought a house in the valley to flip. This was the same day she sold her home and bought the condo. I helped her move from the house to the condo. We lived in the condo, where her son would sometimes stay with us. We were working on the flip house and found out there was a lot more major work to be done and that it would take longer than we originally planned. As we were standing there in the kitchen of the house, looking out the window at the back yard, she said, "I really miss the yard and the trees." We both realized that condo life, surrounded by asphalt and parking lots, was not for us. We decided to move into the house while we finished it and sell the condo. This was also helpful as we were now down to one mortgage payment.

I had a partner on the house whose credit was a problem, so everything was in my name. He had put in a couple hundred dollars, so I paid him that money when we moved in. He was short that month, so I also loaned him $4000 cash. Prior to that I had let him put a $50,000 lien on the flip property so he could be approved for a high-risk loan to buy a real estate business, with the understanding it was a loan and that he was responsible for it. He hoped to pay most of it back from profits on the sale of the house. Unfortunately, there were more expenses than we planned, and we lost $3000 on the home when it sold. I could have lived with that, but there was still more than $40,000 owed on his loan plus the $4000 I loaned him, and now he refused to pay it back. That is an ongoing lawsuit, and it added stress to my new relationship. In the past, I would have been angry at the situation and fumed over it for months. Now I used tools I learned in training, Mainly, I did not focus on him but focused on the action itself. I did not worry about the past action but focused on the present solution. Step by step, I made offers to remedy the situation. He rejected all offers and suggestions. The final step was to take him to court, and that is where we are now. I no longer harbored anger but simply moved to the next step. We moved into that home in October and worked on the house.

During this time, my wife remembered something interesting. She had learned to scuba dive with her son so they would have an activity to do together. At one point, she had taken him to Florida on a diving trip. The divemaster who was guiding them did a phenomenal job, and they had a lot of fun. When it was time to leave, my wife had asked him if he knew anyone back in Utah who could work with them on diving. He answered that he knew a guy who had taught his instructor course and was really good. She couldn't remember the name of the person her Florida divemaster had given. Then one day it came to her, and she realized it was me. It felt almost prophetic. In March I retired from law enforcement, and we got married a week later. We also continued working on the house and finally sold it in August to a nice couple and moved up to the cabin while we built a new home in Hurricane, Utah. The new home was finished in December, and we moved again.

Between us we have six kids. In the first two years we were together, we moved four times, built a home, had two kids get married, had one graduate high school and start college, had two graduate college, had two grandchildren born, and had two children get divorced. All of these can put a great deal of stress on a relationship, and we survived all of them because we talk. I told my wife about all of the things I had seen at work over the years, often crying as I did so. When I shared these incidents, I discovered that many still hurt, but not as bad as they once had. Writing about these events for this book added another layer of acceptance, and the pain decreased even more. I started having fewer PTSD issues. This technique is called journaling and is used by many therapists working with those who suffer from PTSD. This allows us to reframe the events that affect us and change the way we look at them.

My nightmare sequence has shifted over the years, but it is still very real. I know the faces, and I know the stories, because they are victims in cases I have investigated. That backpack was my life, holding me down with its weight because I wouldn't open it up and share the feelings I had. I told myself I was tough, that I didn't need help. I insisted I could handle it, and besides, no one would understand so it was pointless to try. But naturally, bottling things up simply led to PTSD, which contributed to two divorces. I opened that backpack up during my third marriage, and what a difference it has made. I floated free from those burdens. Yes, the dream sequence at the beginning of the book is real, as are others, but I don't have them as often or as graphically since I have shared the burden with a counselor, my wife, and friends.

My wife and I talk about everything. We still have hiccups in our relationship, just like anyone else, but neither of us avoid the problems. At the same time, we know what works to tackle a problem. Great relationships don't mean you don't have disagreements or never get mad. But in healthy relationships, both partners know how to communicate honestly, respectfully, and fairly. So, neither of us shuts down, and neither of us hides. We talk about it. Talk about it and work it out, talk about it and hug it out. I can see an interesting difference in myself and in the success of our relationship as we love, laugh, and live.

CHAPTER 30

THE FINAL SAY

Like Dr. Gilmartin's book *Emotional Survival for Law Enforcement,* my book takes us on the journey of a police officer, from idealistic rookie to cynical veteran and back. Today's world has also added the term *resilience.* Dr. Stephanie Conn, another officer turned psychologist, talks about this quality in her book, *Increasing Resilience in Police and Emergency Personnel.* Both are excellent books and well worth the read.

Resilience is the ability to cope with things, in spite of setbacks. It is also a measure of how much one is willing and able to overcome obstacles to reach an objective. Some people call it "emotional strength." Experts say that resilience is built upon five pillars: Self-awareness, mindfulness, self-care, positive relations, and purpose. Resilience is important as we shift and use problems as learning experiences. Thinking this way allows

191

us to move forward, changing the way we do things to lead us to success without emotional baggage.

My journey was a combination of emotional survival and resilience, the focus of the two books, but with some variations. By being resilient, my journey turned from a slow steady build-up of cynicism like water trickling into a bucket, and instead became a series of ups and downs like waves in the ocean. I rolled back and forth, from idealism to cynicism to idealism and back again. Each step of cynicism built upon the past and continued to increase.

In my career, I started as the idealistic academy graduate, ready to change the world, who was then thrust immediately into a hostile training situation. I quickly became the cynical rookie who justifiably could not trust some of the veterans, just like a scene from the movie *Training Day.*

This was followed by a good chief and a second chance allowing me to get back to being an idealistic, I-can-make-a-difference rookie as things improved and went well. But again, the distrust and cynicism returned as the same group of officers tried to influence my path and career through the second field training.

The cyclical pattern continued as I became a solo officer and things on the job went so well that I quickly moved into Detectives. Then another wave hit, along with another learning curve, as I got another bad (in my opinion) supervisor overseeing my efforts in Detectives.

Being resilient, I remained positive through most of that time. Then another downturn hit as my first marriage deteriorated and I got the negative results of testing for promotion. Preparing for the testing and the potential was a positive experience but being passed over thirteen times took its toll and was definitely a negative. I was really hurt when I found out that the one person who blocked my promotion and spoke out against me was one of my first sergeants and now a captain who I considered to be my mentor. He used one experience from fifteen years earlier to prevent me from being promoted.

The final straw was working a part-time job at Utah Transit Authority Police. For the first time, I had only one part-time job in addition to my full-time job and was financially secure. Then the administration claimed I had lied about the paperwork, when they were the ones who had forgotten the agreement.

This time, I stood up for myself and made a choice that worked for me. I took my retirement and moved on.

For the first three years at UTA, I was on an upward swing. I used my skills as a firearms instructor and first aid/CPR instructor and made myself valuable to the department. I was definitely on the upward rise of the wave.

My first years at Transit were a lot of fun, and I pushed myself in the new world. I pushed to get extra duties and gave whatever I could to the department. I was rated as one of the top three officers in the department for years two, three, and four. Then, in the fifth year I started going through my second divorce and lived at my cabin alone. I was also put onto a brand new, specialized team. Then the report-writing issues started, and no matter what I did I was told it was wrong. Now the downhill slope had begun again, and it was frustrating when I could not seem to stop it. Then I was put on probation and removed from all the jobs I had done so well. My second divorce was final. I was reinstated to my jobs and started dating my new wife.

Now it is time to move on, on my terms. I retired and now onto a new beginning.

My journey was not one big, smooth cycle from idealistic rookie to cynical veteran. Rather, it was a series of smaller cycles from positive to negative, idealism to cynicism, and back again, much like the waves of the ocean lapping at a shore. In this case, the shore was my ego. I was resilient enough to resist and stand firm. But even the smallest waves, if there are enough of them over the years, will have a corrosive effect, turning the sharp distinct edges of our being into worn and rounded humps. Our strength is eroded away, slowly but steadily. PTSD sets in, we build walls and quit talking, we become bitter and feel betrayed. Many of us turn to alcohol or prescription meds for the aches and pains earned in too many foot chases and fights. We get divorced, and some of us take the last resort, suicide.

Luckily, law enforcement and public safety aren't just one large rock but are an entire shoreline. It is still eroding away little by little from within, as described above. And now that shoreline has been subjected to the added negative public pressure and criticism.

If we don't put enough positive energy into the shoreline, the negatives will wear us down and knock us out, one rock at a time, until we are depleted, and the entire shoreline has eroded away and changed.

This is happening right now under our watch as we lose good officers in great numbers. These officers have given and given, and administrators, civilians, and society aren't doing anything to rebuild and strengthen the eroded walls of emotions and trust that have worn away—hopefully not beyond repair. Together we must build a bridge to repair the communication and relationships that have eroded away. Bridging that gap is the only way. This book was written to coincide with the program I teach. It gives tools to work through PTSD which will hopefully reduce divorce and suicide among our public safety personnel.

As public safety personnel are able to rebuild their lives, we can begin to rebuild the relationships in our communities at large. It is a ripple effect, like throwing a stone into a still pond. As our relationship with ourselves improves, our personal relationships improve. Next the relationships near us improve, and the ripples spread exponentially, creating better relationships within our community at large This all starts with open, honest communication.

Part of communication is listening. But regardless of which side we are on, I do not see anyone listening. The talking points are often based on false narratives, and we as a country have allowed emotions to cloud our judgement. I see such a lack of respect in daily discourses that create even more divides, even within the police community. Listen, listen, and listen, then speak openly, honestly, and respectfully. Just like in our personal relationships, we can disagree yet still support each other.

I am fortunate to have been given another chance and am enjoying the uphill rise to the crest of the wave. Now I look forward to the ride without trepidation, much like a surfer. I also look forward to the downside, because that is where my greatest learning opportunities have occurred. I love talking, feeling, and being with my wife, holding nothing back. It is nice to know that I actually contribute to a real relationship, bridging that gap in communication instead of building walls that erode or destroy my progress.

The next and last chapter has a list of resources from meditations online to psychologists who were once police officers and who understand what we see and deal with on a daily basis.

CHAPTER 31

CONCLUSION

Whether you are a new recruit or a grizzled veteran, I wish you luck in your law enforcement career and in your personal relationships. My hope is that you will be open to learn from the mistakes I and others have made. I heard a lot of this information as a young officer and felt it did not apply to me, so I chose to ignore it. I was arrogant, thinking I wouldn't fall into those traps. I did, and I ended up divorced.

Later in life, I learned that personal accountability is one of the most important qualities we can have, and how to stop building the walls I had created. Getting rid of misperceptions and judgments is also very important. I was good at blaming things on my first wife's depression or my second wife's anger and how she ran around with other guys, but when I look at my life deeply and with personal accountability, I get to ask myself, "What did I do to contribute to both failures?"

While it's true that my wives made their own mistakes and ultimately have to take accountability for their behaviors, I can and do take accountability for my own behaviors and contributions (the only thing any of us can take accountability for). In both cases, I shut down and quit talking. I talked about things on a surface-level but never got deep and never talked about how I felt or how different experiences affected me deeply. I opted out of the relationship completely in my first marriage. During the second marriage, I was learning and working hard to save it even though there were warning signals early on that it wouldn't work. I was forgiving about this situation, as was she, and we are actually still friends today. I learned to personally embrace the concepts of responsibility and accountability.

At its most basic definition, the word *accountability* simply means the ability to account for one's choices or actions. The term *responsibility* means the ability to respond to the actions or choices of another person.

As first responders we often fall into a habit of using responding behavior rather than making accountable choices. We are regularly dispatched to a call, then respond and take control. Or we might see something illegal happening in front of us, so we respond and take control of the situation. If a suspect chooses to engage with a certain level of force, we respond appropriately according to what they do. If they throw a punch, we go hands on or use a taser. If they pull a knife or handgun, we respond appropriately, often with deadly force. We respond day in and day out, year after year, until we no longer truly make decisions—even in our personal lives. We simply become first responders. When we are told to be proactive in our jobs, we simply begin responding to something at an earlier stage, recognizing the preliminary indicators and responding before or as it happens rather than after the fact. Responding becomes a habit and slowly encroaches into our personal life outside the job. We simply become responders to our own family, responders to those we love.

But in our personal relationships, simply responding means we aren't making accountable choices. We aren't choosing, but rather we are simply responding to the choices of others. Even today, when my wife asks me what I would like for dinner I periodically slip into response mode and simply say, "Whatever you want is fine with me." I must remind myself to make accountable choices and to be accountable for the choices I make. It is time to take back the power I have so freely and frequently given away. It is time I choose to live.

Being a law enforcement officer is no longer my life. It is a job that I did to make a living and to take care of my family. It is a job that I did to make a difference in my community. It is a job that I loved, but it is a job and not my life.

Make an accountable choice. Choose yourself and your family. Choose to be accountable for your actions and choices rather than wasting lives and relationships by simply responding. Take an active role in your own life. Simply responding is an easy out for the human psyche. In the 1890s, Russian physiologist Ivan Pavlov discovered the nuances of conditioned responses. Pavlov predicted his dogs would automatically salivate when food was placed in front of them. It was an automatic, unconditioned response. He soon noticed that his dogs would begin to salivate whenever they heard the footsteps of the assistant who regularly brought them food. This was a learned and thus conditioned response.

Just like Pavlov's dogs reacted to food, we as first responders react to disaster, violence, crimes, emergencies, or the actions of other people. Then when we get home to our personal lives, we do the same: simply respond, instead of choosing to make accountable choices. We have subconsciously learned that leaving the choices to others makes it easy to have no accountability for those choices. This just happens to be a way to save our own human ego. Making critical, life-or-death choices day in and day out is exhausting, mentally and emotionally. Many times, when we get home, we don't want to make any more decisions. This can feel like a way to avoid being accountable for the result, which in reality we created by not making a choice.

In my first marriage, my wife became depressed. I responded and "hung in there" for eight years to "take care of the kids." Looking back, of course with the benefit of 20/20 hindsight, I should have pushed for medical assistance. But instead, I simply responded to solve the immediate problems. I took on extra jobs and worked more to fix the financial loss, took on cooking and cleaning to take care of the kids, and took the kids to their schools and activities to be the image of a good father. I never once looked at the underlying problem of depression or illness, and I never once made a choice that really worked in the long run.

The second marriage started as a response. I was lonely and responded to the overtures and advances of a woman who wanted and offered affection. After we were married, I responded to her emotional outbursts and temper. I responded to her activities at home. I went to spin classes and other activities that I enjoyed but really only attended passively. I simply went along, never once making a personal, accountable choice. That would have required open, honest, accountable communication. When we finally did have that kind of communication it was too late, and then it was an easy choice. The lifestyle she wanted did not work for me, and we got divorced.

My third marriage has been different. We started with open, accountable communication. We talk. We have made choices that have not worked, but we work through them. Sometimes, when we talk about things that are difficult or were my problems in the past, those old feelings come up. I start to get nervous as my gut tightens from past experiences. I then start to "combat breathe," regain control, and get "back in the fight." I get back into life, and we work things out.

In many ways I am just like Pavlov's dogs who still salivated when they heard the footsteps, even though there was no food. My heart rate still goes up and my eyes scan around for threats or danger when I hear sirens, even though I know I am no longer responding. And the old relationship responses still kick in when old cues arise. I now make a conscious, accountable effort to reduce that stress, to make a choice rather than my old habit of simply responding. That is why my current relationship is working when those in the past failed.

You, too, can make accountable choices instead of simply responding. Responding is a habit, and for some people it is difficult to overcome. You can be the difference in your personal relationships, which will ripple out into your work, and into the city or county or jurisdiction where you work.

This is a personal choice.

I am the difference, and you can be the difference too.

CHAPTER 32

TOOLS

T here are many tools that can be used to prevent the experience of traumatic events from becoming PTSD and negatively affecting relationships. These tools aren't a big secret; in fact, many are common and are useful for creating a healthy mental and emotional life. Are these hard and fast solutions? No, they aren't, because every person deals with traumatic experiences differently. But exploring these tools and picking the ones that work for you can reduce the negative effects of traumatic events.

The following are all tools that have worked for me.

JOURNALING

Journaling, also known as "expressive writing." is one way to stay in the moment, working through the problems that affect you. Write about the incident, including your thoughts and feelings about it. Write the feelings that arise within when you think about it. Figure out what the trigger for those feelings is, and where it occurs. These journaling sessions can be useful, because writing can improve your coping skills. Journaling can reduce PTSD symptoms like tension, anger, or anxiety and has even been shown to decrease flashbacks. If you are in therapy, these journal entries can be used between you and your therapist to guide treatment.

I like to break down a traumatic event and reword it in a self-accountable manner. This makes it possible to share the event with my spouse without creating trauma for them as well.

1. Write the event down in all of its detail. Then write it again.
2. Share the event with someone you trust. Read what you wrote, and ask them to simply listen.
3. Rewrite the event accountably. Simply write what *you* did. Leave out the traumatic details and speak to what you did. For example, (from "The Red Door"): *I ran from my car to the door. As I ran, I called on the radio for backup and drew my weapon. I ran through the door and saw three people fighting. I grabbed one and pulled him away. I grabbed the suspect, threw him to the ground and put handcuffs on him.* This exercise allows you to remove all judgments.
4. Write it again, take accountability, and add how you felt during each step.

I can share steps three and four safely with my spouse or other people in my life. Sharing this way removes any walls to communication and allows me to share without traumatizing others.

Some other tools recommended by many therapists and in many articles, include the following (in no particular order):

HEALTHY LIFESTYLE

Having a healthy lifestyle is important for anyone. But for those with PTSD-related stress and relationship problems, a healthy lifestyle is imperative.

A) **Eat a Healthy Diet:** Diet is such an important part of our life, but when working variable shifts it can be difficult to maintain. Cut back on fast food that we so regularly rely on in our profession. Bring healthy snacks and food with you. You must make the judgment call about what is healthy for you, and this doesn't mean you have to change everything you do, go to a fad diet like keto, or give up all of your favorite things, but watch the amounts you eat.

Shift work can be detrimental to good eating and exercise habits. Both are necessary for good health. The following are some beneficial ways to help improve your diet during shift work:

1. Have healthy foods available at home and at work. People who are fatigued and sleepy are more likely to seek out quick, unhealthy foods. Having healthy options readily available allows us to consciously make healthy choices. This will also help you to be more productive.

2. Bring your own food to work. You are more likely to eat healthy foods that you brought from home rather than finding them at restaurants or in the quick takeout food from the local drive-through. Also, choices are extremely limited late at night, making it even more difficult to find something healthy.

3. Eat small, frequent meals rather than large heavy ones. Heavy meals, like most restaurants prepare, will have more calories than we need. These large portions can also cause a sluggish or tired feeling when you are on the job.

4. Try to eat in line with a regular day. It is difficult to stick with a healthy diet if we eat late at night or throughout our shift.

5. Sit down to eat. Take a break, pause, and eat at a relaxed pace. Eating rapidly and on the go can encourage mindless snacking. I know this is not always possible in the public safety profession but do it as often as possible.

6. Drink plenty of fluids. Our bodies signal thirst and hunger in the same way. Take a water bottle to work and refill it often. This will not only save you money on bottled drinks but is healthier for you. You can flavor the water with commercial packets or simply add citrus slices.

B) **Avoid Alcohol and Drugs:** My years as a patrol officer and detective allowed me to see the effects of alcohol and drug abuse on families and individuals. I also had a stepdaughter who became addicted to pain meds and later turned to heroin when the pain meds were gone. These things scared me so badly that I would not take pain meds, even after a serious rotator cuff surgery and other procedures. But without thinking about it, I turned to alcohol after my divorce. It took me a few months to realize I was depressed. Studies have shown that since alcohol and drugs are depressants, they only make the symptoms of PTSD and depression more severe. PTSD can cause intense anxiety, intrusive memories, and flashbacks that interrupt daily life. This doesn't mean you shouldn't have a cocktail now and then, but if you find yourself drinking every day or craving a drink, it is time to seek addiction counseling.

C) **Take Time to Relax:** Most officers I know forget to take care of themselves. We spend our lives helping others. We forget that if we aren't whole, we cannot help others be whole. Taking time to relax is an important part of our self-care, and it is not selfish to want to be in good mental health. Relaxing can entail a lot of things and is different for each individual. Take time to read a book, go for a hike, go fishing, take a motorcycle ride, or just take a nap. These are all things I have done that take my mind away from work or the unpleasant memories that pop into my head. What works for you is up to you. Try some things that are outside your comfort zone. I have also done yoga and used Tibetan bowls. In yoga, the movement and stretching along with the quiet tones of music aids in the relaxation. The Tibetan bowls create a vibration and tone that moves me into a type of hypnotic trance. I have experienced great insights and total relaxation using this method. When I was a young officer, I would not have considered either one of these techniques, but they have been very beneficial for my self-esteem and relaxation.

D) **Exercise:** Exercise is another key ingredient to physical and mental health. Doctors recommend that we exercise thirty minutes a day. It is easy once the habit is created but extremely easy to get out of the habit and sometimes difficult to start again. Exercise helps us stay in shape, control weight, and maintain fitness. All of these things are important to the safety and wellbeing of law enforcement and public safety personnel. A side benefit of exercise is the creation of endorphins in our body. Endorphins create a feeling of ease and clarity. This affects our mood, since it reduces stress, and we feel good. As mentioned before, I went to marriage counseling because I wasn't communicating with my wife, and the counselor suggested that my wife run with me because I open up and think clearer when I exercise. The counselor was right. The time I spent exercising was also the time I would be most likely to open up and talk.

Exercise can be a form of mindful meditation and can also create focus. Some examples of exercise include running, walking, bicycle riding, or doing exercises that have a repetitive movement of the entire body including martial arts. Tai Chi in particular creates focus on one specific part of the body at a time. Surfing has been shown to be beneficial as it requires being in tune with and connecting nature with the movements of your body. Again, there are an infinite number of possibilities. The key is regular, daily participation in one or more activities.

E) **Get Plenty of Sleep:** Getting plenty of sleep (between seven and nine hours a night) can be difficult when working variable shifts or being on call and having sleep interrupted, but sleep is imperative for both our physical and mental health. Think about the decisions you have made when you are fatigued and sleep deprived. This happens to a lot of officers, since we work extra shifts or extra jobs to provide for our families. Studies have shown that too little sleep can result in weight gain. Sleep deprivation also slows reaction time, and we tend to communicate in a much less respectful manner. Remember, if we are not healthy, we cannot really help anyone else.

F) **Mindfulness:** Mindfulness simply means taking a moment to be aware of one's body and feelings. One important thing I learned in my self-enhancement training (that has also been emphasized by my current wife) was how to be in the moment. To me this means being totally conscious of what is happening right now, both within my body and mind as well as around me externally. The past does not matter; it cannot be changed. Use it as a reference to learn from. The future does not matter, since it depends on what I do right now. This means I must focus on this moment, right now, and give it one hundred percent. Take care of yourself. Mindfulness is a broad term that can be part of many activities from meditation, yoga, aromatherapy, relaxation massages, and many others. Mindfulness assists you in being aware and living in the moment, the here and now. The goal is feeling and focusing on the now. (I now go in for massages regularly and do meditation exercises regularly. These activities not only take away physical discomfort but take off the mental edges that lead to anxiety or stress.)

H) **Be of Service.** Many officers feel that they live to be of service to their community. This is true but serving in this capacity is our job and that is the main reason we do it. We are often required to go above and beyond the call of duty; however, there are actually mental and physical health benefits to being of service outside of work. There are seven benefits of service that most counselors seem to agree upon: 1) Reduces stress 2) Combat's depression 3) Prevents feelings of isolation 4) Increases confidence 5) Gives a sense of purpose and meaning 6) Ignites passion 7) Makes you happy.

Does this service have to be a big, time-consuming project that makes the news? No, simple little acts also provide the benefits of service. In the past I have given Christmas donations to a needy family or showed up at the home of a stranger in need, with a nice meal for their family. An easy thing I've done before is to simply pay for coffee for the car behind me in the coffee shop drive-through.

G) **Social Support:** Your social support can be a spouse, significant other, friend, support group, or even a therapist. Find someone you are comfortable with who will not judge you, will listen without trying to fix it, will allow you to work through it, and will allow you to be honest about what you need and want. Talk about your feelings and experiences with someone, as many times as it takes.

Other well-known treatments that have been found to be successful include the following:

Eye Movement Desensitization and Reprocessing (EMDR) Therapy: EMDR has been recommended by several people, and I have used it myself. It is an interactive psychotherapy technique used to relieve psychological stress. It has proven to be an effective treatment for trauma and post-traumatic stress disorder (PTSD).

I have also used Rapid Eye Technology (RET) which is very similar to EMDR. RET is a technical and spiritual model that releases trapped trauma and stress and brings the body into balance. When the body is in balance, anything that is out of balance inside begins to release, whether it is physical, emotional, mental, or spiritual. One part of the process is rapid eye blinking, with verbal input. The movement from light to dark to light to dark creates a state of balance and will allow feelings of trauma and stress to be released.

RET combines eye movements with verbal input to release the trauma. This process is done with a doctor or therapist.

Cognitive Processing Therapy (CPT): In CPT, you begin by talking about the traumatic event with a therapist and how your thoughts related to that event have affected your life. Then you write in detail about what happened. This process can help a person look at the way they think about the traumatic event and figure out other ways to live with it. In most cases this process takes several weeks.

If a person is blaming themselves for something, the therapist can help them take into account all the aspects of the incident that were beyond their control, so they can move forward. They can then understand and accept that, deep down, it was not their fault, no matter what they did or didn't do.

Prolonged Exposure Therapy: If a person has been avoiding things that remind them of a traumatic event, prolonged exposure therapy will help them confront the event. It usually involves several sessions.

Usually, the therapist will teach you breathing techniques to ease anxiety when you think about the event. Then you will make a list of the things you have been avoiding in life and learn how to face them, one by one. In another session, you will recall the traumatic experience to the therapist, then go home and listen to a recording of them.

Doing this as homework over time can help ease your reactions to the event that you experienced.

Here's a quick recap of the possibilities for treatment:

Eye Movement Desensitization and Reprocessing Therapy
Cognitive Processing Therapy
Prolonged Exposure Therapy
Activities that can assist in treatment:

Journaling

Talk/Social Support

- **Spouse**
- **Friend**
- **Coworker**
- **Peer support group**
- **Therapist**

Exercise (at least half an hour daily)

Meditation

A good therapist or support group is a must. There are many therapists out there who have been in law enforcement and are now working to assist officers and their families deal with life on the job. I know and trust the following groups and counselors:

Building Warriors: This is a peer-run nonprofit group of public safety counselors who provide direct services and training to emergency responders, healthcare professionals, and others who experience traumatic events and experiences.

Andrea Brown: Andrea Brown is a clinician serving Eagle, Summit, and Grand counties in Colorado, specializing in substance abuse, PTSD, trauma, and mental illness. She also does video conferencing for law enforcement professionals outside her area. Andrea has a master's degree from Regis University in Criminal Science and Human Behavior and a master's degree in Addiction Counseling. Andrea is a Certified Addiction Counselor II and holds a Level I National Certification. Andrea has had extensive training in areas involving addiction, domestic / sexual violence, crisis intervention, and managing traumatic incidents. Andrea works with adult individuals, families, and provides group treatment for court ordered offenders.

Andrea moved to Colorado in 2006. As a former sworn law enforcement officer, her passion is to provide service to first responders from both peer based and therapeutic perspectives. She is a certified CIT officer in both Utah and Colorado. Her 12-year law enforcement relationship brought her to Building Warriors to fulfill a dream of providing quality treatment and support to those who put the well-being of others before themselves in first responder roles.

Andrea Brown MS, RP, CAC II, NCAC I
(970) 406-2620
andrea@buildingwarriors.org

Global Trauma Response Centre: This group can be found online and is made up of trained Trauma Debriefers. Many who can assist in taking the edge off of a traumatic experience. Many of these are retired first responders. Since this is a worldwide group, the sessions are available 24/7 and are conducted on a secure zoom channel. You can find them and sign up for sessions online by googling the global trauma response center or contact the author on his website for information.

BLUE H.E.L.P.: It is the mission of Blue H.E.L.P. to reduce mental health stigma through education, advocate for benefits for those suffering from post-traumatic stress, acknowledge the service and sacrifice of law enforcement officers we lost to suicide, assist officers in their search for healing, and to bring awareness to suicide and mental health issues.

Blue H.E.L.P. has a list of resources online that are accessible and confidential for first responders:

Code 9 Project: Code 9's mission is to provide education, support and viable self-help tools to all Public Safety Personnel and their families for the purpose of managing and reducing the compressive stress effects, such as PTSD and suicide.

Code 9 Project also has a confidential peer support group. Google Code 9 Project meditation and you can find meditations that work for you. There are many options.

There are a lot of other organizations out there to assist officers, both active and retired, with emotional or PTSD problems brought on by the ongoing trauma of the job. These are just a few that I have built contacts with over the years.

I actually wrote my program, "Bridging the Gap," in 2015 but allowed my own fears of failure to delay its final development. Since then, many others have established programs to deal with PTSD and suicide and the effects on first responders' lives and relationships. In each program I see pieces of what I originally wrote and am in wholehearted agreement with them. I began the final development of my own program in 2018, and this delay validated to me that I am on the right path. Instead of regretting the delay, I chose to move forward. Now I travel and teach "Bridging the Gap, an Inside Look at Communication and Relationships" to public safety professionals in the hopes of reducing PTSD, divorce, and suicides. The final piece of my project is this book.

The moral to this story is that we all have the power to change ourselves and improve the ways we communicate and live. We have the power to work through the effects of PTSD. If we cannot do it alone, we now have resources available to help us work through it to improve our lives and help us survive the turmoil within. We have the power to choose. I chose to move forward and continue making a difference, not just in my own life, but hopefully in the lives of those I meet, train, and who read this book.

You can make a difference too. It starts with making a difference in your own life. The difference in you will then ripple out to your family's lives, and then out to lives of the communities where you work and reside. These changes will affect anyone you come in contact with. It all starts with you. I've heard the words "I tried," but only from those who failed. Don't try. Step forward, give all you've got, and like the old Nike commercials say, *just do it*. I know you can, and I believe in you. You are strong enough to be a public servant, and you are strong enough to be your own master and overcome the things that are negatively affecting your life and relationships.

GOOD LUCK IN YOUR LIFE AND KNOW, YOU'VE GOT THIS.

ABOUT THE AUTHOR

 Glen Williams spent twenty-six years in law enforcement working as a patrol officer, detective, and trainer at Sandy City Police and Utah Transit Authority Police and has PTSD. He has conducted trainings throughout the United States for law enforcement and civilians in scuba diving, police and evidence diving, underwater post-blast investigation, firearms, patrol rifle, active shooter response, and first aid/CPR. He has coached individuals in personal self-discovery and self-development. Glen received a bachelor's degree from the University of Utah in Psychology.

Glen has had articles published in the Utah Peace Officer's magazine, appeared on local television and regularly attends and presents at public safety conferences and conventions and currently travels to police departments throughout the US presenting his program, Bridging the Gap: An Inside Look at Communication and Relations to assist with reducing PTSD, divorce, and suicide.

After retiring in 2016, Glen now lives in Draper, Utah. He enjoys traveling to Florida to enjoy the ocean and beaches with his wife Deborah. Glen and Deborah have six children spread across the western US and enjoy visiting them and spoiling the grandchildren. Glens greatest joy is making a difference in today's world through speaking, teaching, and writing. He also enjoys traveling, scuba diving, martial arts, long range shooting, and his dog, Shiloh, who goes most places with him.

BONUS

Follow Glen on his web site glenwilliamspublicspeaker.com. You can schedule Glen's 8-hour course, also titled Bridging the Gap, by contacting Kate O'Donnell at Public Grants and Training Initiatives at 847-875-3620.

Look for Glen's upcoming books, "A Sweet Life: Growing up and Growing Old with Diabetes and an action-adventure series featuring Thomas Grey-Eagle, a Scottish/Native-American detective who prevents the destruction of the government of the United States.

A free ebook edition is available with the purchase of this book.

To claim your free ebook edition:

Visit MorganJamesBOGO.com
Sign your name CLEARLY in the space
Complete the form and submit a photo of
the entire copyright page
You or your friend can download the ebook
to your preferred device

Print & Digital Together Forever.

Snap a photo

Free ebook

Read anywhere

Printed in the USA
CPSIA information can be obtained
at www.ICGtesting.com
JSHW022326140824
68134JS00019B/1326

9 781631 955686